A Wind Swept
Over the Waters

A Wind Swept Over the Waters

Reflections on 60 Favorite Bible Passages

John Nichols

Skinner House Books
Boston

Copyright © 2007 by John Nichols. All rights reserved. Published by Skinner House Books. Skinner House Books is an imprint of the Unitarian Universalist Association of Congregations, a liberal religious organization with more than 1,000 congregations in the U.S. and Canada, 25 Beacon St., Boston, MA 02108-2800.

Printed in the United States.

Cover design by Kathryn Sky-Peck
Text design by Suzanne Morgan
Text illustration *The Sea*, © 2000 Caren Loebel-Fried, www.carenloebelfried.com
Cover art *Knight Pond #2* © 2005 Irma Cerese, http://ceresearts.com/

ISBN 1-55896-527-0
978-1-55896-527-0

09˙08˙07
6 5 4 3 2 1

Library of Congress Cataloging-in-Publication Data

Nichols, John, 1943-
  A wind swept over the waters : reflections on sixty favorite Bible passages / John Nichols.
       p. cm.
  ISBN-13: 978-1-55896-527-0 (pbk. : alk. paper)
  ISBN-10: 1-55896-527-0 (pbk. : alk. paper) 1. Bible--Meditations.
I. Title.

BS491.5.N53 2007
242'.5--dc22
                                    2007008890

All Bible passages are quoted from the New Revised Standard Version except 1 Kings 19, which is quoted from the Revised Standard Version; Psalm 100, which is quoted from the New King James Version; and Hebrews 11, which is quoted from the King James Version.

The Unitarian Universalist Association is committed to using gender-inclusive language in its publications. In the interest of accuracy, quoted material is presented in its original form.

This book is dedicated to
Daisy, Gaia, Naomi and Dylan

I have not made it through all my trials alone, and I appreciate the reassurance that these lovely words bring.

As our lives change, even the most familiar words of the Bible can strike us in new and unexpected ways. Many of us were brought up to believe that a scriptural passage can have only one meaning. This idea limits our appreciation. Reading the Bible is more like looking into a spiritual mirror. When we really absorb its language and images and give ourselves time to let them work their way into our souls, the ancient words can touch our life experience in unexpected ways.

Because everyone's life experience is different, no two people will understand or be affected by scripture in the same way. I believe many of the passages reflect a message so profound that they point to the divine, but the text is also mediated, first translated into words that people of the writer's time could understand and then filtered again through a new context for contemporary readers.

The writers of the Bible often use metaphors, expanding the ways we can appreciate it. In Psalm 23, the writer refers to God preparing "a table before me in the presence of my enemies." Taken literally, these words describe the writer preparing to enjoy a banquet while surrounded by envious antagonists. But the metaphorical meaning is deeper and wiser: the psalmist feels like an honored guest in God's house even though, like all of us, he has enemies.

Preface

Words, images, and stories from the Bible haunt us. Whether we are Christian or not, churched or unchurched, liberal or conservative, scriptural stories and images reverberate throughout our culture. They maintain a powerful hold on the hearts and imaginations of many of us, whether we see them as the word of God or as classic literature.

In this book, I set aside the question of what Bible passages "mean" because, for the most part, we don't know. That discussion is interesting but perhaps not as important as why certain passages keep a tenacious influence on how we understand what it means to be human. When we tackle that question, we encounter a power in the scriptures that transcends theology.

When I was a hospital chaplain, patients asked me to read Psalm 23 to them more than any other passage: "The Lord is my shepherd, I shall not want." I was a young man then, and I couldn't quite comprehend the powerful attraction of these words. I could not imagine wanting to be made to "lie down in green pastures" or to be led "beside still waters." I didn't want to imagine myself as that dependent. Now, in what I hope is a time of greater maturity, I know

CONTENTS

The passages at the end of this book are from Jesus' parables. A parable is not simply a story with a moral. Nor is it a fairy tale beginning with "Once upon a time" and ending with people quite unlike us living happily ever after. A parable is an ordinary story about ordinary people or events, in which something dramatically strange and different happens, something that is at first difficult to understand. The story will not let us go until we have wrestled with it, and its meanings begin to work their way into our lives.

Jesus' disciples reacted to his parables as many of us do. We want the teachings neatly wrapped and packaged. Most scholars believe that Jesus did not attempt to explain his parables. Instead, he tried to get his followers to think very differently about the life of the Spirit and the quality of human relationships that he called the "Kingdom of God." I'm not sure I have correctly interpreted the parables—or any of the passages, for that matter—but I promise that I have wrestled honestly with them and invite you to do the same.

Most of the Bible passages are quoted from the New Revised Standard Version. With the exception of the parables appearing at the end, the passages are presented in the order in which they are found in the Bible. To arrange them in any other way would present my categories and theology as the central theme of this book. In fact, the reader will look in vain for a coherent theology; I don't have one. Yet this book reflects what I believe deeply and hope to live by.

My primary object in writing, however, is to be provocative enough to start you on your own journey, one that leads you into a deeper, more profound relationship with these ancient words and images.

A Wind from God Swept
Over the Face of the Waters

In the beginning when God created the heavens and the earth, the earth was a formless void and darkness covered the face of the deep, while a wind from God swept over the face of the waters. Then God said, "Let there be light"; and there was light. And God saw that the light was good; and God separated the light from the darkness. God called the light Day, and the darkness he called Night. And there was evening and there was morning, the first day.

GENESIS 1:1–5

Something powerful and mysterious is going on behind creation's scenes, and it is described here as a wind sweeping over the face of the waters. Because we have difficulty picturing God, who is grand yet also subtle and elusive, we tend to imagine God in tangible ways. We think of God as a person. But this passage describes an experience. We experience "something more" in our lives long before we are able to understand what happened and long before we struggle for the words that describe it.

"A wind from God swept over the face of the waters." Imagine you are in a canoe drifting on the surface of a lake or a bay. Suddenly a breeze comes up, the waters swell and the scene is alive with energy. Something is happening, but what? There is movement everywhere, but you cannot define it. You cannot paint its picture. You can only imagine what it sets into motion.

A wind can blow hot and cold. It can bring relief but it can also challenge us. It comes and goes, and everything moves with it. It brings storms and dry spells and the world is nurtured by it. Life depends on this wind sweeping over the waters, transforming and changing everything. *God* is the word we use to describe an experience that, like the wind, is powerful and mysterious, present sometimes and sometimes seemingly absent, intimate, challenging, endlessly creating, and absolutely unavoidable.

People often say that at one significant turn in their lives they received a push, which helped them make a difficult decision or encouraged them along a hard but vital path. Who or what pushed, they do not know. They do know they have many reasons to be grateful for an impulse that came from somewhere and then moved on. Let us hope for the wisdom to know when we are being pushed and moved.

Indeed, It Was Very Good

God said, "See, I have given you every plant yielding seed that is upon the face of all the earth, and every tree with seed in its fruit; you shall have them for food. And to every beast of the earth, and to every bird of the air, and to everything that creeps on the earth, everything that has the breath of life, I have given every green plant for food." And it was so. God saw everything that he had made, and indeed, it was very good. And there was evening and there was morning, the sixth day.

GENESIS 1:29–31

God has been creating up a storm: heaven, earth, beasts, birds, flowers, trees, women, and men. Then God leans back for a longer view of the work at hand and thinks, "Oh, this is very good." But the real question is what are we to make of God's work—life with its high and low moments, its subtleties and complications. The gift is in embracing life without reservation, so that others can see how we value the life we've been given.

Life is good, but what about violence, war, and senseless tragedy, not to mention mosquitoes, lice, and the flu? What about the pain that good friends carry around with them? Tragedies can happen to all of us. Sadness sometimes visits a life so often it seems to make a home there. Yet we have friends who rise above their own difficulties and affirm such strength for living that we look to them as ship captains used to look to lighthouses on foggy nights.

These friends keep us from breaking up on the rocks. They have balanced the good with the bad, the really wonderful with the awful so that they see the goodness in their lives as a generous if mysterious gift. They see every rough moment as a challenge to be met rather than an insult to be grieved. Their rugged optimism enables them to affirm that life is very good despite the sadness they may have known, despite threats real and imagined, despite the ignorance, malice, and injustice that seem to be all around. Life is good because the gifts we have been given can sustain us through the losses that will inevitably come.

Many speak of this kind of optimism as if it were either an unrealistic response to the world or an unattainable one. A person who is consistently upbeat may be called a "Pollyanna," as if that described someone who was resolutely child-like, refusing to view the world as it really is. It is much more likely that when we are resilient in the face of inevitable disappointments, we have made a conscious decision to focus on the unearned graces in our lives rather than on what we think we "deserve." Resilience is a refusal to keep score of our gifts and our losses, because we know we have been given so many gifts that we have not yet begun to recognize and appreciate them all and we never will.

Life is very good not because we refuse to recognize its dark moments and tough challenges, but because we know we can rise above them.

You Must Master It

Now Abel was a keeper of sheep, and Cain a tiller of the ground. In the course of time Cain brought to the Lord an offering of the fruit of the ground, and Abel for his part brought of the firstlings of his flock, their fat portions. And the Lord had regard for Abel and his offering, but for Cain and his offering he had no regard. So Cain was very angry, and his countenance fell. The Lord said to Cain, "Why are you angry, and why has your countenance fallen? If you do well, will you not be accepted? And if you do not do well, sin is lurking at the door; its desire is for you, but you must master it."

GENESIS 4:2–7

This is the story of a man who is tormented because he believes that he does not have the blessing he should have. We don't know why Cain's offering is not as pleasing to God as Abel's, but it doesn't matter. The causes of sibling rivalry are many and varied. Some parents really do prefer one child over others. It's normal. Some siblings will always feel injured though no one else can ever find or repair the injuries. The issue isn't always who's right. The problem is there cannot be enough external approval in the world to satisfy everyone's need for it.

Most of us want and need to be cheered on. We want to be told when we've done good work. More than that, we want to believe we are a little bit special, perhaps even more special than others. Comparisons are inevitable, and we make them all the time. Rivalries —real or imagined—are the major cause of bitterness between people in families and institutions. They create heartache and tensions that radiate far beyond the lives of the people involved.

What do we make of God's response in this story? Recognizing that Cain is upset, God reminds him, "If you do well, will you not be accepted? And if you do not do well, sin is lurking at the door; its desire is for you, but you must master it." This isn't quite what Cain wanted to hear, because, as we learn later, he lures his brother out into the fields and kills him.

God's rhetorical question, "If you do well, will you not be accepted?" is almost Buddhist. If we are as true to ourselves as we can be, using our gifts to their greatest advantage, regardless of the rewards or who gets them, then we will feel a sense of accomplishment. We will find both acceptance and peace. If, like Cain, we are drawn to needing ever more recognition and praise, then "sin is lurking" at our door. Our need for constant applause will be the source of our pain and unhappiness, which is why we "must master it."

I Will Not Let You Go
Unless You Bless Me

The same night he got up and took his two wives, his two maids, and his eleven children, and crossed the ford of the Jabbok. He took them and sent them across the stream, and likewise everything that he had. Jacob was left alone; and a man wrestled with him until daybreak. When the man saw that he did not prevail against Jacob, he struck him on the hip socket; and Jacob's hip was put out of joint as he wrestled with him. Then he said, "Let me go, for the day is breaking." But Jacob said, "I will not let you go, unless you bless me." So he said to him, "What is your name?" And he said, "Jacob." Then the man said, "You shall no longer be called Jacob, but Israel, for you have striven with God and with humans, and have prevailed."

GENESIS 32:22–28

9

It's hard to like Jacob. He deceived his father and cheated his brother, Esau. To escape Esau's wrath, Jacob found his way to the land of Laban, a kinsman, where he fell in love with Laban's younger daughter, Rachel. Laban agreed that Jacob could marry Rachel if he put in seven years of hard work. Seven years later, on the morning after their wedding, Jacob woke up to discover that the veiled bride he had gone to bed with was none other than Rachel's older sister, Leah. "Oh, didn't I tell you?" his father-in-law asked when confronted. "It's a custom here that we always marry the older sister first. But you can marry Rachel if you will work for me for seven more years."

Jacob worked seven more years and married Rachel as well while Laban became a wealthy man on the strength of Jacob's efforts. Eventually it became clear to Jacob and his wives that they would never be free of Laban's control. One day they packed up and slipped away, taking the better part of Laban's flocks and some of his jewelry. This time there was nowhere to flee but back to the brother who Jacob cheated more than twenty years earlier. After getting started, they learned Esau was waiting for them with four hundred men.

Afraid he would get the reception he so justly deserved, Jacob sent several of his flocks and shepherds ahead of him as a peace offering. Then he sent his two wives and many sons forward to soften Uncle Esau up. That night, Jacob waited alone on the far side of a swift river that separated him from his brother. There he wrestled until daybreak with a mysterious stranger. Whether he actually wrestled with his conscience or God, we don't know nor do we know if, after a life of shady dealing, he finally regretted cheating Esau.

Sometimes, perhaps at night before sleep, we turn an issue over and over looking for some clear resolution, some "aha" moment when the correct answer suddenly arrives. But often the answer does not come to us. There is no "right" choice that gives us confidence. Life is full of junctions where we must choose among equally unconvincing alternatives and then go on. The ability to choose and move on is critical for everyone. What happens when we make that decision may not be insight or conversion, but it is the courage to take responsibility for our lives despite the frailty of our knowledge and the inconsistency of our wisdom. The ability to do so is a blessing—the only real blessing we need—and with that blessing, we limp off into the future like Jacob.

At the end of this passage, Jacob is given a new name, because he has "striven with God and with humans" and has prevailed. One thing is clear. Jacob has "striven" with himself, and his new name reflects a new identity grounded in greater clarity and control over his ambitions and temptations.

I Am Who I Am

Then the Lord said, "I have observed the misery of my people who are in Egypt; I have heard their cry on account of their taskmasters. Indeed, I know their sufferings, and I have come down to deliver them from the Egyptians, and to bring them out of that land to a good and broad land, a land flowing with milk and honey, to the country of the Canaanites, the Hittites, the Amorites, the Perizzites, the Hivites, and the Jebusites. The cry of the Israelites has now come to me; I have also seen how the Egyptians oppress them. So come, I will send you to Pharaoh to bring my people, the Israelites, out of Egypt." But Moses said to God, "Who am I that I should go to Pharaoh, and bring the Israelites out of Egypt?" He said "I will be with you; and this shall be the sign for you that it is I who sent you: when you have brought the people out of Egypt, you shall worship God on this mountain."

But Moses said to God, "If I come to the Israelites and say to them, 'The God of your ancestors has sent me to you,' and they ask me, 'What is his name?' what shall I say to them?" God said to Moses, "I AM WHO I AM." He said further,"Thus you shall say to the Israelites, 'I AM has sent me to you.'"

EXODUS 3:7–14

Having fled from Egypt to escape punishment for killing a slave driver, Moses took up the quiet life of a shepherd. One day, while he was alone in the mountains, a bush burst into flames. He knew immediately that God was in the fire, for a voice told him that he now stood "on holy ground." God had seen the sufferings of the Israelites and told Moses to go to Egypt and plead with the Pharaoh to let the Israelites go. Moses wondered why the Israelites would follow him, of all people, and so he asked for a sign, a name that would give him credibility with them. God responded, "I AM WHO I AM."

What's in a name? Why do we ask for them? If someone tells you his name, he gives you a way to get his attention. He tells you something about himself and offers what could be the threshold of a closer relationship. He dispels some of the mystery of who he is and implies that he may give up even more of that mystery as your acquaintance deepens. The God of this passage is not going to do that, not then, not ever. Moses and the rest of us will have to get used to the idea that God is radically, mysteriously, and beautifully different from anything we can shape, control, or even describe, and that is how God remains free from being defined (and therefore not limited) by us.

We can only hope that once in a while, and likely when we least expect it, we will find ourselves "on holy ground." There may be no burning bush in those moments but we will, as a result, become more sure of who we are and more confident of what we must do. God leads not by becoming more attractive or visible to us, but by becoming unavoidable. I AM WHO I AM or, as it is sometimes understood, I WILL BE WHAT I WILL BE.

The Israelites finally sought their freedom not because they knew God would hold their hands, leading them safely past all danger and then making everything right, but because they believed they had to do it. Something finally unavoidable compelled them to leave the comparative securities of slavery for the freedom and terror of the wilderness. As it turned out, God's five-word self description really meant, "I am who you must confront."

When those confrontations arise, when we are asked to do what is difficult but right, something crucially important to our future integrity and happiness happens. May we recognize this even if we don't understand why.

You Shall Not Make
for Yourself an Idol

Then God spoke all these words: I am the Lord your God, who brought you out of the land of Egypt, out of the house of slavery; you shall have no other gods before me.

You shall not make for yourself an idol, whether in the form of anything that is in heaven above, or that is on the earth beneath, or that is in the water under the earth. You shall not bow down to them or worship them; . . .

You shall not make wrongful use of the name of the Lord your God, for the Lord will not acquit anyone who misuses his name.

EXODUS 20:1–7

The ground shook. Lightning lit up the sky, and a dark cloud hovered overhead. Something awesome was about to happen. And the first words out of that thundercloud are not words of overwhelming power or threat. They are words of love. God tells the Hebrew people in effect, "I brought you out of the house of slavery, and now I will show you how to stay free." The story of the Ten Commandments is about freedom and how to keep it.

Why should we worry about idols today? Because we have neither outgrown nor given them up. We create and worship idols all the time, and then we allow them to enslave us. They become the ends for which we live, our definitions of fulfillment and success. One individual may pour her energies into building or furnishing a house, hoping that this house will provide the sense of completion she has been missing elsewhere. Or a parent may idolize a child, not the real child, of course, but a vision of what that child may accomplish, thereby bestowing her parents with prestige. All too frequently, we idolize the reigning symbols of power or status and commit ourselves to a path that will appease them.

As creations of our own anxieties, these idols may not easily let us go, and they often leave us feeling we haven't yet paid them enough tribute. We can spend our lives doing penance because we believe we haven't served them sufficiently. We have not worked hard enough or long enough or have not accomplished enough to keep our idols happy. No relief or forgiveness is ever entirely in sight.

What does it mean to love or worship God instead of craving the more flattering gods of our insecurities and pretensions? It would mean responding to what Quakers call an *inner light*, an inner compass or a sense of direction that feels right because we recognize that our thoughts keep coming back to it while we pursue other goals. God's path is often the road we have not yet taken because we have been tempted to try more seductive ways.

We can make that choice, however, and take that road, fulfill our truest hopes and dreams, honor the people who have made our lives meaningful, and repay some of the debt we have accrued by living. We can claim our freedom by passing up those idols that offer a false comfort. Freedom, after all, is really finding the courage to do what seems right and true rather than being harnessed to anxieties about fame, power, and security. God does not demand a six-figure income, power, popularity, or fame. God asks that we live honestly, generously, and with integrity, which may be what the passage means by worshiping God only and not idols.

Living free of idol worship is a lifelong struggle that is never completely won. It is, however, an effort that establishes our freedom and integrity in an all too seductive world.

Remember the Sabbath Day, and Keep It Holy

Remember the sabbath day, and keep it holy. Six days you shall labor and do all your work. But the seventh day is a sabbath to the Lord your God; you shall not do any work—you, your son or your daughter, your male or female slave, your livestock, or the alien resident in your towns. For in six days the Lord made heaven and earth, the sea, and all that is in them, but rested the seventh day; therefore the Lord blessed the sabbath day and consecrated it.

EXODUS 20:8–11

Slaves don't have days off. The Hebrews knew that. They worked continuously in Egypt and were granted respite only because their masters did not want to kill them, but to get the most work out of them. After they escaped, wandered through the Sinai wilderness, and secured their freedom, some probably continued to work relentlessly. It was their habit. They valued nothing else. Slaveries of all kinds can be mysteriously addicting since they offer the simplest answers to questions of what to live for and how to set priorities.

How do we stop being slaves and enjoy being free? The Hebrews wondered about this on Sinai. Like them, we can try to stop laboring toward goals that offer little satisfaction because they are not our goals. How did we get enslaved in the first place? Perhaps we are enslaved when we value our hopes, dreams, our self, and our time so little that we give our freedom away to some cause that seems to make better use of it than we think we could. The Hebrews found that escaping Egypt was only the first step in gaining their freedom. They then had to find something to live for that made freedom more meaningful than slavery.

One way of understanding this commandment to honor the Sabbath is: God got tuckered out from working hard for six days in a week so who are you to think you can work seven? Another way of hearing the passage is: God wants us to shut everything down once a week so that we can give thanks and praise for all that God has done for us. I prefer to hear it this way: God takes you very seriously; perhaps more seriously than you take yourself. God believes that you know more than you think you do about the strengths you have and the purposes for which you live and who you have to thank for this incredible life.

Therefore spend time at least once a week—observe a Sabbath—in which you take your freedom, your truest hopes and dreams, and the very real threat of self enslavement seriously, and then decide what you should be doing with your life. Keep that time holy. In that moment, after you have divested yourself of the tensions that arise from all of your other commitments, you may meet yourself and you may find God.

Honor Your Father and Mother

Honor your father and your mother, so that your days may be long in the land that the Lord your God is giving you.

EXODUS 20:12

We have complex relationships with our parents. We hear what sounds like a criticism or complaint from Mom or Dad, and we become children again. If this commandment is taken to mean that we should *obey* our mothers and fathers, then we are really conflicted, because the very idea of obedience threatens our independence. Actually, if we even hear *obey* implied in the word *honor*, it is a reflection of how often the thought of our parents carries us back to feeling like children. There is a better way to understand what it really means to honor someone upon whom we are no longer dependent.

If we attended a banquet to honor Coach Jones, who taught generations of soccer players, we wouldn't feel obligated to do wind sprints just because the coach said so. We would be there to pay respect to a complex individual who taught us useful and important disciplines. We would acknowledge what the coach did best and how his life has influenced ours, but we might also laugh a bit at his foibles and quietly recognize that he had some qualities that were not so nice. Everyone has a dark side. In maturity, we learn to weigh the good with the bad and honor the good wherever possible. This holds true with our parents as well.

But the commandment promises that if we honor our parents we will live a long time. It means our lives will be long in the quality of our days and our relationships. Accepting that our parents did the best they could with the strength and wisdom they had available to them not only makes it possible for us to make peace with them, but it also opens the door for us to accept our own limitations—in the raising of children and in everything else.

Everyone struggles to create a meaningful life, and the energy we have to care for others is limited. It must come out of that same pool of energy by which we earn a living, keep a house, and hold our own demons at bay. Our energy for life varies from day to day, even from moment to moment. At different times in their lives, our parents also had greater or lesser energy for parenting.

If once we expected them to behave as the gods and goddesses of our world, then as adults we must honor that they simply did the best they could with the energy and wisdom they had available. Even as we assess our strengths and weaknesses and take responsibility for what our lives become, we owe our parents an appreciation for who they are and what they struggled to achieve regardless of who we may have wanted them to be.

When children and parents can live without feeling guilty toward one another and the independence of parent and child is established, then the days of each can be longer and happier on the earth. And when children watch how their parents treat their grandparents they will learn that respect links the generations. They will understand that a healthy family honors the separateness and togetherness of its members, with forgiveness all around.

Choose Life

Surely, this commandment that I am commanding you today is not too hard for you, nor is it too far away. It is not in heaven, that you should say, "Who will go up to heaven for us, and get it for us so that we may hear it and observe it?" Neither is it beyond the sea, that you should say, "Who will cross to the other side of the sea for us, and get it for us so that we may hear it and observe it?" No, the word is very near to you; it is in your mouth and in your heart for you to observe. . . . . I call heaven and earth to witness against you today that I have set before you life and death, blessings and curses. Choose life so that you and your descendents may live.

DEUTERONOMY 30:11–14, 19

Moses was 120 years old when he addressed these words to the people with whom he had shared a wilderness journey of forty years. It was his birthday, and God had told him he would not be allowed to lead his people into the Promised Land. These were men and women with whom he had shared the greater part of his life, his hopes and dreams, but they were about to cross the river and reach their goal without him. They gathered to receive his final blessing, and he told them they must "choose life."

One way to approach this passage is hear the emphasis on the word choose. To realize and keep the freedom they had been given, they were going to have to make thoughtful choices. This must have been hard for them to hear, because they had little experience with choices. Even when given the freedom (and peril) of the wilderness they kept hoping someone else would choose for them. And so, very often, do we.

We live too much by established habits and predilections. We may not remember whether we chose them or they chose us, but when we leave our comforting routines, the ground underneath us seems to tremble. We know we are entering territory with new uncertainties, and yet we must go there because thoughtful choices infuse our lives with energy. Letting things just happen fills us with boredom. Choosing wisely confers life and commitment to something worthwhile, but finding a comfortable groove helps us avoid choosing and leads to a dulling of our spirit.

In one of his poems, Robert Frost describes a man who came to the junction of two wooded roads, and he took the one less traveled knowing that through his choice—through every serious choice—he was altering his life in a way that could never be rolled back. The poet tells this story "with a sigh" as if we all hate it that such irrevocable choices must be made. But he also comments that choosing a road less traveled is what has "made all the difference."

A thoughtful choice, by its very nature, is a powerful investment of our energy. If we often fail to choose, we invest little and we get little in return. Before us, then, is the chance for a life in which we give ourselves to what energizes us or a life in which we accept what comes most easily. If we choose—rather than let our choices be made for us—we increase our chances for exciting and meaningful lives, and those who follow us will be encouraged by the choices we have made.

A Still Small Voice

And he said, "Go forth, and stand upon the mount before the Lord." And behold, the Lord passed by, and a great and strong wind rent the mountains, and broke in pieces the rocks before the Lord, but the Lord was not in the wind; and after the wind an earthquake, but the Lord was not in the earthquake; and after the earthquake a fire, but the Lord was not in the fire; and after the fire, a still small voice. And when Elijah heard it, he wrapped his face in his mantle and went out and stood at the entrance of the cave. And behold, there came a voice to him, and said, "What are you doing here, Elijah?"

1 KINGS 19:11–13

For an awesome moment such as God speaking, we expect at least a choir, accompanied by the earth shaking, strong winds blowing, and a sky full of incredible colors. That's the way it happens in the movies, but it is not what happens for us in real life. If we wait for the wrong signs, we could miss God's voice when it comes.

Elijah, the prophet who is the subject of this passage, faced that possibility. He thought God had commissioned him to orchestrate a show of strength against two corrupt rulers and those who served them. He put on an incredible magic show reflecting the power of God. Elijah thought he had made his point and carried the day; feeling victorious, he expected some sort of reward. However, he only succeeded in antagonizing the king and queen, who sent back word that he was about to have a very short life. Elijah was so disappointed he hid in a cave and wished his life would end sooner rather than later. Eventually he was addressed not in any of the ways he had expected but by a "still small voice."

What is a "still small voice"? It is less than a whisper but more than sheer silence, making the silence around us feel like something about to burst with meaning. It is a thought that prowls around the edges of our consciousness, a nagging thought we cannot get rid of, a thought we finally have to wrestle with to gain its fullest meaning. Maybe it isn't a thought so much, but a feeling that comes to us out of left field, a feeling that conveys assurance or acceptance or even pardon just when we need it most. Perhaps it comes as a "voice of conscience," which makes us uneasy about the gap between what we profess and what we do.

We do not know for sure what is behind that voice, which is not even a voice so much as a thought, but perhaps there have been certain times in our lives when that nagging thought has been unmistakably if indescribably there. Our experience of being addressed in some way is the source of both theology and poetry. In the end, we do not come much closer than this passage does, suggesting there is something that quietly, insistently wants our attention. We may not ever understand this still small voice completely, but we do need to pay attention.

Why, O Lord, Do You Stand Far Off?

Why, O Lord, do you stand far off?
>Why do you hide yourself in times of trouble?
In arrogance the wicked persecute the poor—
>let them be caught in the schemes they have
>>devised.
For the wicked boast of the desires of their heart,
>those greedy for gain curse and renounce the Lord.
In the pride of their countenance the wicked say, "God
>>will not seek it out";
>all their thoughts are, "There is no God."

PSALM 10:1–4

The psalms are cries from the heart. They affirm that God is present in the beauty and bounty of creation and in our lives. At the same time, they lament that God is too often absent from our daily lives and because of that absence, evil prospers. Why, in a creation so incredibly well fashioned, do malice and avarice flourish? Why does justice so often fail? These passages, in their wonderful and brutal honesty, reflect the joy of God's presence and the pain of God's absence. They affirm faith, but doubt is also a legitimate companion.

The world that this passage describes is like a poorly supervised playground. It is recess, and children spill out of the building. A teacher is present, but he is far from the action. Perhaps he is reading a book or gazing off into space. Seeing no adult effectively in charge, the larger children begin to harass and intimidate those smaller. Fights break out. Lunch money is stolen. Those who feel most vulnerable huddle together, because they fear being picked off one by one. It's hard for them to understand why no one has stopped the fighting. It is hard in that situation to have respect for authority. Translate all of this into the world of adults who can do much more damage to each other. That is what the psalmist decries in this passage.

Something about the question of God makes us feel like vulnerable children waiting for an adult authority to provide protection. But perhaps we've got it wrong. God's intent is not to punish the people we think should be punished. Rather, it is to fill us with a hatred of injustice so that we will curb the strong and protect the vulnerable. God's role is not to divert hurricanes, prevent automobile accidents, or stop bullets, but to flood enough hearts with compassion so that together we survive both natural and humanly contrived disasters.

Is God in hiding as the passage says? Naturally, we wonder about this but perhaps God is present in our impulse to wonder and then recognize that we must lend our weight to the struggle for a just and compassionate world.

On some days, this sense of God working through our best efforts will be enough to sustain us. On other days, we will say in our own words what is said in this passage. That may well be the inescapable dilemma of attempting to live faithfully in this world. We will always wonder why God does not keep the world in better order—and then we will return to doing our part.

Day to Day Pours Forth Speech

The heavens are telling the glory of God;
    and the firmament proclaims his handiwork.
Day to day pours forth speech,
    and night to night declares knowledge.
There is no speech, nor are there words;
    their voice is not heard;
yet their voice goes out through all the earth,
    and their words to the end of the world.

PSALM 19:1–4

This passage offers us a paradox, and the writer wants us to know that the words in this passage have been carefully chosen. The heavens are "telling" of God's glory. The earth "proclaims" God's work. Day "pours forth speech" and night "declares knowledge." There seems to be a lot going on. But then we are told, "There is no speech, nor are there words; their voice is not heard." Then, "Yet their voice goes out through all the earth." The last two verses are so dramatic they seem to say that we have got to notice this. We must get it.

We long for God to speak, to give us a word or two of comfort, encouragement, or direction. Sometimes even criticism would be welcome if only we heard something to demonstrate God's presence. There is no voice that is not our own. For some people, that silence settles the matter. If there is no voice, there is no God. But this passage reminds us emphatically that God is speaking all the time, and evidence of that speech is everywhere. We hear no voice that is not human. Yet sometimes, when we most urgently need them, we sense that messages of encouragement and hope are coming to us from a world that reflects God's glory and promises. This is the premise of the following vignettes.

Imagine a woman who is deeply pensive about something and unable to sleep. She finally gets up at 3:00 A.M. to pace the floor, brew coffee, eat, read, do anything to distract her from what is really keeping her awake. Her thoughts are racing, colliding with each other in fear and confusion. She does not know how she will get through the next day or two.

By 5:00, however, the early rays of the sunrise begin caressing everything around her and catch her attention. She watches, fascinated by the show, forgetting for a moment that it is the new day she dreaded. The more she watches, the more she realizes that fear's hold on her is diminishing. This new day will not be entirely awful, and there could be a better day after that and then another. The bleakness painted on her internal landscape is overmatched now by the simple promises of the world, which brings freshness every morning.

A hiker stands on the summit of the state's tallest mountain. The haze has not yet risen from the valleys and he can see clearly the progression of lower ridges and fields marching away from him toward the sea. The sun seems to hit each ridge or field differently, illuminating more hues of green, yellow, or blue than he ever thought possible. Though he occupies higher ground than any other individual in the state and has worked hard to get there, he does not feel superior to anyone. In that moment, something says to him, "You belong in this world. You are part of all this. Welcome home." There is, of course, no speech. But something speaks words that no one hears.

Winters in New England are often long, cold, cloudy, and damp, with only intermittent relief. Spring comes slowly, almost imperceptibly, and the first signs are often crocuses, small violet flowers that poke their way through the thawing soil to signal the coming of new life. They will get covered once or twice by a late season snowstorm, but, as they have foretold, the snow does not prevail. Creation is on the move again and it will not be stopped. The voice of the heavens "goes out through all the earth and their words to the ends of the world."

In the 1930s, some French pilots based in Algeria brought a group of Bedouins to Paris to show them the wonders of modern Europe. These hard-bitten practical Arabs were not impressed with the trappings of Western power. Locomotives, automobiles, airplanes, the Eiffel Tower did not move them particularly as anything more than symbols of commotion and dirt. What did leave them absolutely astonished was a waterfall. They were transfixed by it. They would not move away. They kept waiting, they said, for the waterfall to stop, as surely it must. God, whom they had learned in their own lands was very stingy with gifts, would not allow this waste of water. It was a symbol of life's crazy, endless bounty. "The heavens are telling the glory of God, and the firmament proclaims his handiwork."

Even Though I Walk
Through the Darkest Valley

The Lord is my shepherd, I shall not want.
    He makes me lie down in green pastures;
he leads me beside still waters;
    he restores my soul.
He leads me in right paths
    for his name's sake.

Even though I walk through the darkest valley,
    I fear no evil;
for you are with me;
    your rod and your staff—
    they comfort me.

You prepare a table before me
    in the presence of my enemies;
you anoint my head with oil;
    my cup overflows.

Surely goodness and mercy shall follow me
all the days of my life,
and I shall dwell in the house of the Lord
my whole life long.

PSALM 23

All of us have walked through dark valleys. We are likely to do so again. When we get an unexpected phone call or when a loved one is overdue returning on a stormy night, we wonder if yet another dark valley awaits. These are our most intimate moments when we are driven to the final measure of strength. That is why in this moment in the psalm, the passage stops talking about God in the third person and begins speaking to God directly, "I fear no evil for you are with me. Your rod and your staff—they comfort me."

The change is so dramatic that we feel it before we even know what we are hearing. We yearn for this intimacy with God and wish we always shared the certainty of knowing that God is with us.

In a mood of desperation, the psalmist begins to talk to God, to pour out his or her heart to God with all of the anger and fear that anyone feels when walking through a dark valley. God's response is very different from what the psalmist experiences from friends. God does not attempt to explain why this terrible thing is happening. God does not suggest solutions. God does not rationalize. God does not suggest, "You'll feel better tomorrow." Somehow, in the midst of a mind-shattering catastrophe, the psalmist feels that the awfulness of the situation is fully understood—though how is almost too intimate to explain. The psalmist feels accepted, and that acceptance strengthens him or her. God does not promise that awful things will no longer happen. God says that no matter what does happen, the courage to go on living will continue to be there and will be lovingly offered.

We can walk through our personal catastrophes just one step at a time. Often, if we keep going, the strength to survive them is there when we need it. Pieties and pep talks and all forms of advice are frequently no help at all. What we really need is a gentle push forward, because the whole point is that we are going *through* that valley. We are not going to stay there. We are going to come out on the other side. We will not dwell in darkness. This much is assured.

The Net and the Rock

My eyes are ever toward the Lord,
for he will pluck my feet out of the net.
Turn to me and be gracious to me,
    for I am lonely and afflicted.
Relieve the troubles of my heart,
    and bring me out of my distress.
Consider my affliction and my trouble,
    and forgive all my sins.

PSALM 25:15–18

To you, O Lord, I call;
    my rock, do not refuse to hear me,
for if you are silent to me,
    I shall be like those who go down to the Pit.
Hear the voice of my supplication,
    as I cry to you for help,

as I lift up my hands
toward your most holy sanctuary.

PSALM 28:1–2

We think of a net as a rescue device for trapeze artists and sailors, but there was a time when nets were used by combatants to disable the opposition. Anyone who has ever tried to climb out of a net can appreciate how it works. The more stress you put on one strand of the net, the larger the hole you create, possibly falling through if the hole gets large enough. It is easy to get confused as to where to put pressure and where to ease off in order to get a firmer purchase that will make escape possible.

The net the psalmist is talking about is really self-woven, and many of us have been caught in it. When we build identities based on lies, evasions, or impossible hopes, we build a net that will not let us go. There is no truth in it. There is no hard place upon which we can put our weight to leverage our way out of our trap. We need help in order to get free, and that help may be the power of honesty rushing into our lives and into our relationship with God.

By contrast, Psalm 28 speaks of God as a rock. When we encounter rocks in gardens or lawns, we think of them as inanimate objects that should be removed. However, anyone who has ever been in a massive flood would feel differently. The ground that had once been firm and predictable becomes so saturated with water that it slides underfoot and cannot be trusted. What had once been reliable becomes fluid. Only large rocks can be trusted to withstand the force of the water-soaked ground.

There are times when we need to put our weight down on something firm in order to escape traps and floods. That hard place may be our conviction that certain things are right and true and worthy of our loyalty. It may also be an intuition, a still small voice that tells us where our resting place must be. It may be our willingness to accept on faith that the experiences that others reflect in their cherished writings are worthy of being taken seriously.

When we are caught in a moral dilemma in which no decision seems altogether right, we say we are between "a rock and a hard place." Sometimes, particularly in moments of moral confusion or identity crisis, this is not a bad place to be. If the rock is a conviction that will not let us slip and slide away from important commitments, then it may help us define for ourselves who we are and what we believe.

We'd do well to understand where our rocks and hard places are and what they suggest for how we live the rest of our lives.

What Is the Measure of My Days

Lord, let me know my end,
    and what is the measure of my days;
    let me know how fleeting my life is.
You have made my days a few handbreadths,
    and my lifetime is as nothing in your sight.
Surely everyone stands as a mere breath.
    Surely everyone goes about like a shadow.
Surely for nothing they are in turmoil;
    they heap up, and do not know who will gather.

And now, O Lord, what do I wait for?
    My hope is in you.

PSALM 39:4–7

Could we endure knowing the measure of our days? Imagine a conversation between a doctor and her patient:

"Tell me, Doc. I can take it. How long have I got?"

"Well, I make it ninety-two days and three hours, give or take the change to daylight savings time."

Imagine how we might spend those ninety-two days if we faced that prognosis. We probably would grieve the time we will miss out on. We might be angry that life has been cut short. We would hope the prognosis is wrong. We might count down the days with a feeling of dread darkening every one of them.

There is one more possible response. We could try to squeeze as much life as possible out of every day. Every subsequent hour would become twice as valuable as it was before. Knowing how little time remains, we might recognize how precious people are to us; how miraculously beautiful are the trees outside our windows; how absolutely unique and pregnant with meaning is every moment and how very grateful we are for all of this.

We are so intoxicated with getting things done that we miss much of what happens to us every twenty-four hours. We are so desperate for love and appreciation that we do not recognize it when it is actually offered. We are in such a hurry to get on with our lives that we miss much of what real life holds out. Would you rent a videotape and then insist that it be played only on "fast forward"? That's the way many of us live. One day we have toddlers demanding to be fed and changed, then suddenly they are teenagers demanding the car. Whoops. How did that happen? One day we feel physically indestructible, the next we encounter serious limitations.

Let us drink in as much life and meaning out of every day as we possibly can. If it takes reminding ourselves that there is an actual end to our days on earth, then the reminder can only help us to stop and savor the gift that is fully ours for as long as our lives last.

Be Still and Know that I Am God

"Be still, and know that I am God!"

PSALM 46:10

Because his parents had taken him to several different religious services, he thought he knew what to expect. But this Quaker worship service was different. Rather than chattering amongst themselves while waiting for the service to begin, people entered and sat quietly. No one spoke for fifteen minutes. It was just too much for one six year old, so he stood up suddenly and spoke from the heart. "Who is in charge here?" he demanded.

Extended silence among friends or colleagues makes most of us anxious. We wonder if someone should break the silence and be "in charge" rather than let the leadership go unresolved. As the silence lengthens, the person who minds it most will break it first, often with an anxious remark. This is why interrogators often get people to say more than they intended by allowing long silences between questions.

It would be far better if we learned to befriend the quiet moments in our lives by backing down our anxiety about who's in charge and what's going to happen. When we enter into silence, we may be embarrassed, at first, by what's going on in our minds. We will surface very trivial thoughts and even run through "to do" lists for the week to come. It is important for us to follow our thoughts, even our instant reactions, wherever they may lead. With time and comfort, those thoughts will deepen. If we give it a chance, eventually each time for silence will feel like a gift, an opportunity to absorb the world more carefully, a chance to wonder and love. In the calm that comes more readily as we get used to silence, we become less driven by anxieties and regrets. We give ourselves a "time out" for developing a spiritual life.

The psalmist writes, "Be still." Those words could easily be understood as "let it go" or even "get over yourself." As we learn to put aside the worries that haunt our days and nights and our concerns for comfort, status, and security, we enter into a world that is large enough to love us even when we feel unlovable. This world is tender enough to help, hold, and heal us. Be still and know that what we desire the most has been there for us all along, waiting to "speak" out of that stillness.

You Make the Gateways of the Morning and the Evening Shout for Joy

Those who live at earth's farthest bounds are awed by your
    signs;
you make the gateways of the morning and the evening shout
    for joy.

You visit the earth and water it,
    you greatly enrich it;
The river of God is full of water;
    you provide the people with grain,
    for so you have prepared it.
You water its furrows abundantly,
    settling its ridges,
softening it with showers,
    and blessing its growth.
You crown the year with your bounty;
    your wagon tracks overflow with richness.

The pastures of the wilderness overflow,
 the hills gird themselves with joy,
the meadows clothe themselves with flocks,
 the valleys deck themselves with grain,
 they shout and sing together for joy.

PSALM 65:8–13

This psalm is bursting with energy. The psalmist is on fire with gratitude for the beauty and the abundance of the life he or she has been
given. The psalmist imagines that creation literally shouts for joy,
and even those who live at the farthest boundaries of the earth are
enthralled with this power of God. It is a power so awesome that life's
incredible fullness is spilling over for everyone. "The river of God is
full of water." Imagine what that must have meant to someone who
lived in a desert land.

Can you remember the times you were this high on life? Do
your mornings and evenings "shout with joy"? Most of us would
rather our mornings not shout at all since shouting would disrupt
our gathering of wits for the new day. In the evening, no yelling
sunsets, please, for we are trying to get to sleep. We begin and end
our daylight hours semi-awake, and some days we are not all that
alert or appreciative of the hours in between. Babies often wake up

and greet the dawn with shouts of joy, but somewhere along the way of growing up most of us lose the impulse.

It would be a great gift to truly know that every twenty-four hours we are given an irreplaceable opportunity rather than just another mark on the calendar, counting off the days toward a weekend or a vacation.

The passage also speaks in a very intriguing way about the "gateways" of the morning and the evening. A gateway is an entrance or an exit—so each day is presented as a journey from a hopeful start at one gateway to a hopeful finish at another. If we took our days as seriously as we take our journeys, we would stay awake; prepare for them; anticipate the possibilities for adventure, discovery, and surprise; and, perhaps, end up at the last gateway with a sense of completion and hope for the journey to come. Living well is a real challenge for the spirit.

O Sing to the Lord a New Song

O sing to the Lord a new song;
    sing to the Lord, all the earth.
Sing to the Lord, bless his name;
    tell of his salvation from day to day.
Declare his glory among the nations,
    his marvelous works among all the peoples.
For great is the Lord, and greatly to be praised;
    he is to be revered above all gods.

PSALM 96:1–4

Old habits are difficult to break. Destructive habits—such as addictions to food, alcohol, drugs, or work—have rooted themselves in the structure of who many of us are. Just when we think we have fought free of them, we find them still nagging at the corner of our minds. Then we sometimes wonder if we have over-estimated the value of losing them. To break the habit, we must reorder our lives. We need to create a new way of living for ourselves. We often wonder if it can be done.

There are many who could tell us it can. It will not be easy. To imply otherwise would do a tremendous disservice to the members of twelve-step groups who see one another through trials and partial failures as they grow slowly into their new lives. The work is daunting, far more than most people can accomplish through simple willpower. To make such a change, we must believe that the effort of changing our lives is worth making and that we can do it, though we cannot at first imagine where we will find the strength to go forward.

We can sing a new song. We will need help from friends and even strangers. We will need that mysterious strength that comes upon those who in the throes of serious transition find themselves helped to move forward. We will need to take it one step at a time, to celebrate each day until aspects of the person we are becoming crowd out the unwanted traits of the person we have been. Though our family and friends believe they have heard all the tunes that could ever pass our lips, we can sing a new song. This psalm celebrates the miracle of renewal, which comes to everyone who sincerely and honestly seeks it, and we must celebrate as well.

We may never know from where that miracle of personal and spiritual change comes and it may not be important. What is important is that we can learn a new song.

It Is He that Made Us
and Not We Ourselves

Make a joyful shout to the Lord, all you lands!
Serve the Lord with gladness;
 Come before His presence with singing.
Know that the Lord, He is God;
 It is He who has made us, and not we ourselves;
 We are His people and the sheep of his pasture.
Enter into His gates with thanksgiving,
 And into His courts with praise.
 Be thankful to Him, and bless His name.
For the Lord is good;
 His mercy is everlasting,
 And His truth endures to all generations.

PSALM 100

"It's a free country," we say. "I have to be my own boss," some say. When talking about someone who is an individualist, we suggest that she "marches to the beat of a different drummer." We exalt the courage of those who are guided by their own goals and visions, not the desires of others.

In these ways, we are still the spiritual children of Emerson and Thoreau, who made individualism seem romantic. Our earlier spiritual ancestors who believed they literally were the children of God (saying, "It is he that made us and not we ourselves") often seem remote from our thoughts and feelings.

The distance between our understandings and those of our ancestors has been increased as well by shifts in scientific thinking. Not so long ago our forebears believed the first man and woman were Adam and Eve. Many of us now who believe humans are the product of an evolutionary process, which began when elementary molecules mingled. Those of us who accept evolutionary thinking, often find the phrase "He who has made us" sounds like something from a discarded past. Here is where the heavy hand of literalism obscures the truth of poetry.

We are under a self-serving delusion. It is simply not true that we are indebted to no one. Life is an incredible gift. Feeling and expressing gratitude for that gift is essential to our spiritual life and health. Without gratitude, we become completely absorbed by resentment about things that do not always go precisely as we hoped.

We do not make the rules for enjoying this gift. We cannot do without food, water, or oxygen. We cannot abuse our body without serious consequences, and we cannot ignore, without detriment, the requirements of the human spirit.

We need to be treated with dignity and respect, which can happen only if we treat others in the same way. We need the challenge of learning to love others, and we need the security that friendships bring. We need to do meaningful work or to know that our labor creates value for others. Most of us do better when we live and work in a supportive community. The increasing pressure now bearing down upon our lives makes that support even more essential.

Meeting all of those requirements helps bring happiness and purpose to our days. So let us make a joyful noise that Creation or God has given us all the conditions for a wonderful life. We are not self-made, and we know what we have to do to make the best use of the gift of life. If we respect those conditions, we will have the joy that is promised in that gift.

I Lift Up My Eyes to the Hills—
From Where Will My Help Come?

I lift up my eyes to the hills—
    from where will my help come?
My help comes from the Lord,
    who made heaven and earth.

He will not let your foot be moved;
    he who keeps you will not slumber.
He who keeps Israel
    will neither slumber nor sleep.

The Lord is your keeper;
    the Lord is your shade at your right hand.
The sun will not strike you by day,
    nor the moon by night.

The Lord will keep you from all evil;
    he will keep your life.

The Lord will keep
your going out and your coming in
from this time on and forevermore.

PSALM 121

The opening sentence of this passage is a question, not a statement. The question is answered in the next verse: help comes from God, not from the hills to which the psalmist refers.

Many people hear this passage differently, however. They can affirm wholeheartedly, "I will lift my eyes to the hills because there I have always felt loved and supported." They might find it difficult to explain the "why" of this spiritual relationship to the hills, but they would affirm that walking into the hills is unquestionably a powerful experience.

Supreme Court Justice William O. Douglas once wrote of the day during his childhood when his father was buried. Standing by that open grave, feeling desolate and abandoned, he saw the snow-covered summit of Mount Hood in the distance. Majestic and magical in its remoteness, it seemed to promise a sanctuary for his spirit and a healing from a wisdom more ancient than human life itself. Later, while recovering from lameness inflicted by childhood polio, he tested himself over and over against the mountain trails until his body and fighting spirit caught up with each other. He always felt that mountain wilderness was a large part of his recovery.

The mountains are a sanctuary for many. Others seek their private moments near the sea, in the lake country, in the desert, in their gardens, or in a favorite park. We all seek a place where our nagging wants and fears are dwarfed by the power and beauty of a natural sanctuary. We want to go where something larger than our anxieties can quiet the noise in our heads and allow us to listen to the rest of life. We do not "find" God only in the hills or by the sea, as if those locations were exclusively God's home. Instead, God finds us when we are in the place that stills our noise long enough to allow us to hear something beyond ourselves.

How Could We Sing the Lord's Song in a Foreign Land?

By the rivers of Babylon—
    there we sat down and there we wept
    when we remembered Zion.
On the willows there
    we hung up our harps.
For there our captors
    asked us for songs,
and our tormentors asked for mirth, saying,
    "Sing us one of the songs of Zion!"

How could we sing the Lord's song
    in a foreign land?

PSALM 137:1–4

Many situations make us feel that we have been exiled to a "foreign land." We might have moved to a culture so different that it was hard to get adjusted. We may have discovered that suddenly our most cherished beliefs are so radically at odds with those of the people around us that we must keep quiet about them, or if we speak, we must be prepared to defend ourselves.

This psalm is a reflection of what it was like for the Hebrew people to have lived in an exile that was imposed upon them. In 587 BCE Israel was conquered and its leadership was transported to Babylon, where they were permitted to live and work but not to leave. The Babylonians hoped that over time the Jews would lose their cultural and religious identity.

Babylon was an urbane civilization where they worshiped many gods but none seriously. They considered their Jewish captives stiff-necked country bumpkins to ridicule and mock. "Sing us one of those crazy songs about Jerusalem," they asked. This psalm vividly expresses the captives' memory of that experience. The Jewish people remembered, "On the willows there we hung our harps," for "how could we sing the Lord's song in a foreign land?"

Many people live in some kind of Babylon. They live where they cannot speak some thoughts without criticism. To survive in such a negative culture, it is tempting to negate our own convictions as being finally not that important. It is tempting as well to keep quiet, walking away from conversations that might expose our differences. Either temptation sacrifices something of our integrity in order to maintain relationships that will be "safe" though always slightly dishonest. One of the most important spiritual strengths we have is the ability to be honest about who we are.

Recognizing that what was at stake was nothing less than the integrity of their souls, the Jews of Babylon formed communities in which their heritage and their ethical convictions became vastly more important to them in exile than they had been before. They sought each other's support to affirm their differences from Babylonians and to raise their children as if those differences really mattered. Because they chose community rather than safety and anonymity, their convictions survived to make a lasting impression on the world. May we all seek and find the communities we most need in the foreign lands through which we must travel.

I Am Fearfully and Wonderfully Made

I praise you, for I am fearfully and wonderfully made.
    Wonderful are your works;
that I know very well.
My frame was not hidden from you,
when I was being made in secret,
    intricately woven in the depths of the earth.
Your eyes beheld my unformed substance.
In your book were written
    all the days that were formed for me,
    when none of them as yet existed.
How weighty to me are your thoughts, O God!
    How vast is the sum of them!
I try to count them—they are more than the sand;
    I come to the end—I am still with you.

PSALM 139:14–18

Look at your hand. Can you remember how many times that hand has been cut, scraped, bumped, bruised, infected, or even broken? You can't remember, of course. And your hand cannot tell you, because all but the most recent insults have been forgiven. They have healed. That hand has largely restored itself while you protected it from injury. And apart from the effects of growing older, plus your current health challenges, your whole body has done a spectacular job of healing itself every day.

Someone once commented that, given the number of destructive microbes there are in the world, it is a wonder any of us lives a long life. We survive and flourish because our bodies are miraculously equipped to combat most of what tries to attack them. We are wonderfully made.

These words, written by someone with a much shorter life span than we can expect, express profound gratitude for something most people take for granted, the gift of a functioning body. This thankfulness should be the beginning and the foundation for our approach to everything. We are awesomely and wonderfully made. We are indebted to powers that restore us even when we are not completely aware of our need for healing. What a reason to be grateful for each new day!

The Fear of the Lord Is
the Beginning of Wisdom

The fear of the Lord is the beginning of wisdom,
and the knowledge of the Holy One is insight.

PROVERBS 9:10

We think highly of intelligence. Children are tested for it, and parents regard their children's test scores as one indicator of future "success." By contrast, the authors of Biblical scriptures aren't as interested in intelligence as they are in wisdom. Intelligence tells us how to get from Point A to Point B in the quickest, surest way. Wisdom asks us whether we really want to go there.

Wise people are not praised for their quickness of wit. Wit is not important to what they offer us. They offer an unusual ability to draw insight from experience. They build bridges between their spiritual interiors and those of others, and they can cross those bridges, something many people do not do easily. The people we call "wise" remind us how complicated we are and how treacherous is the boundary between What We Can Do and What We Can But Probably Should Not Try To Do. They recognize there are limitations that we need to take very seriously.

The words *fear of the Lord* stand out in this proverbial phrase, because most people today do not want to associate fear with God. Yet the Bible seems to have an uncomfortable fondness for this phrase. How can the fear of the Lord be the beginning of wisdom when many regard fearing God as a superstitious act?

In this passage, fearing God can be understood as recognizing there are limits beyond which we should not go to demonstrate how rich or powerful or clever or popular or cunning we can be. Those limits may be boundaries between our own lives and the lives of others or they may be the limits between us and boundaries that Must Not Be Crossed. If we cross those boundaries, we may violate the rights and feelings of others or we may become so obsessed with our own importance that we lose our good sense and human companionship. Fearing the Lord means recognizing that something is more important and more sacred than exercising our abilities and ambitions.

Fearing the Lord can mean that before we cross into the realm of someone else's life, we need to be very clear about why we are "going there." We should worry about who is best served by what we are intending to do. We should consider whether we are thinking of ourselves exclusively or of others as well.

Ambition is a wonderful and powerful thing. It is important, however, to know where the limits of our ambition should stop, recognizing the legitimate boundaries to our relationships. This fear of God can lead us to a humility which then allows wisdom to enter our lives.

Vanity of Vanities! All Is Vanity

Vanity of vanities, says the Teacher,
    vanity of vanities! All is vanity.
What do people gain from all the toil
    at which they toil under the sun?
A generation goes, and a generation comes,
    but the earth remains forever.
The sun rises and the sun goes down,
    and hurries to the place where it rises.
The wind blows to the south,
    and goes around to the north;
round and round goes the wind,
    and on its circuits the wind returns.

ECCLESIASTES 1:2–6

What is the meaning of life? This seems a silly question because it is impossible to answer. But the author of this passage tells us that he spent many years trying to answer it anyway.

First, he sought pleasure. He spared himself no sensual or sybaritic delight. But his pleasures felt hollow and unconvincing as if he were "chasing after wind." He then threw himself into hard work, and did well at it by conventional standards, but he got no more intrinsic reward from all his labor than those who worked very little. Hard work alone didn't make him a happier person nor give him any feeling of accomplishment.

He devoted himself to righteousness, hoping that God would reward him for being a good person, but he finally decided he was no better off than those who lied to their friends and cheated their neighbors. He sought and won power, more power than most people ever dreamed of having, but it brought him little satisfaction. Finally, he concluded that all of the striving most people do is after rewards, which have no substance. Everything is vanity. Our gains and recognitions, once in sight, often vanish in the air.

The same thoughts challenge most of us, often at the mid-points of our lives. We are tempted by what the world holds out as the conventional routes to happiness. We envy the rich and the powerful and wonder what it would be like to have their lives. We may even try to achieve what we think they have achieved. We envy the popular or the unusually devout and allow ourselves to believe they almost certainly have found the secret to long-lasting comfort. The closer we get to those goals, the more illusory they appear. All is vanity.

Is this pessimism really justified? Perhaps some of the work we do on behalf of others has incrementally made their lives just a little easier. It is even possible that there are institutions or causes that have moved progressively forward because we enlisted our strength in that effort. When we measure our "success" by whether or not it has brought us happiness, we may well be chasing an impossible thing, because happiness is something that comes to us in ways that cannot be measured. If we look at our lives in the light of what we have done to benefit others, then we may find something has been accomplished and we can take some real pride in that.

A life lived for its own ends and purposes alone can be as frustrating as chasing after the wind. And a life enlisted for others probably will not produce the great, just, and compassionate society. It will, however, make an important difference in a world where caring and compassionate efforts do count.

For Everything There Is a Season

For everything there is a season, and a time for every matter
    under heaven:
a time to be born, and a time to die;
a time to plant, and a time to pluck up what is planted;
a time to kill, and a time to heal;
a time to break down, and a time to build up;
a time to weep, and a time to laugh;
a time to mourn, and a time to dance;
a time to throw away stones, and a time to gather stones together;
a time to embrace, and a time to refrain from embracing;
a time to seek, and a time to lose;
a time to keep, and a time to throw away;
a time to tear, and a time to sew;
a time to keep silence, and a time to speak;
a time to love, and a time to hate;
a time for war, and a time for peace.

ECCLESIASTES 3:1–8

This enduring passage reminds us that having to confront sadness and death is part of life's core curriculum. We will always be tempted to lean more heavily on the positive and the joyful, negating any value to pain and sadness. But there will still be times of great personal trial. Some things we cannot get around. Among them are situations so terrible that deep sadness and mourning are the holiest and healthiest responses we can make.

We know this, of course, but the value of reading it again or of hearing it read to us is that these words from an ancient source link us to generations who have walked through those dark valleys and emerged on the other side. They remind us that the strength and patience that eluded us in our worst moments has seemed elusive to people in every generation, yet they survived their own tough times. And there is another very important message in these words: This too will pass.

The passage also weaves this beautiful litany into a longer argument that there really is no such thing as progress. Essentially, it is saying, "This too will pass, but it will come back again, and that's the way our lives always will be." It is hard to accept that there will always be "a time to kill, and a time to heal" and a "time for war." It is not easy to think we may not be able to eliminate the "time for hate" that the passage suggests is just another part of life.

Perhaps there is a time for war. Perhaps there is even a time to hate what erodes the dignity or freedom of men and women. When religious or political movements have tried to perfect the human condition by scourging men and women of their unpleasant qualities, like some of those mentioned in this passage, they have failed in the attempt and sometimes with tragic consequences. Living a full, productive, and involved life is a wild ride, and if we are ready for whatever comes, including our own blind predilections, we will find blessings among the trials and challenges.

For Love Is Strong as Death

Set me as a seal upon your heart,
    as a seal upon your arm;
for love is strong as death,
    passion fierce as the grave.
Its flashes are flashes of fire,
    a raging flame.
Many waters cannot quench love,
    neither can floods drown it.
If one offered for love
    all the wealth of one's house,
    it would be utterly scorned.

SONG OF SOLOMON 8:6–7

Can love be as strong as death? Nothing approaches the influence that death has in our lives. Literature, philosophy, and religion reflect how we respond to knowing we will die. Does that knowledge render all our achievements pointless? Shall we risk investing in friend-ships, families, or falling in love, knowing that finally even our most cherished relationships must end? Isn't much of our drive toward accomplishment and success a futile attempt to contain the wind—futile because, in the end, everything we love blows away?

The answer to all these questions is no. For those who care deeply about people, institutions, or God, love can be stronger than the fear of death. Sooner or later, our lives will come to an end but we need not be haunted because we fear that end. We need not spend all our time attempting to cheat or deny it. When we love someone deeply, we create a bond, a life together, a spiritual life in which our anxiety about ourselves is eased by our attachment to another. We cannot know whether this new life carries on into another dimension after death, but we can know that it sustains us in living and the loss of that courage to live is the death we fear most.

Victor Frankl, who has written about his life as a prisoner in Nazi death camps, remembered that those in the camps who had no strong attachments to other people, to hopes and dreams, or to God, died quickly for they had nothing to believe in but their bodies, which were imprisoned. Those who communed in their thoughts and dreams with someone they loved survived much longer.

Frankl remembered that, while stumbling through a winter's night march, a man walking next to him commented it was a good thing their wives didn't know what was happening to them. Neither knew whether their wives were still living, but Frankl then found himself having a conversation with his wife. The bond they had shared was so strong that he felt she was present with him and neither was imprisoned. Later, he reflected that even if he had known she was dead, their relationship would have been as strong in that moment for the reality their love created was stronger than death. It was a flame that neither water nor flood nor human cruelty nor human frailty could quench.

Here Am I; Send Me!

In the year that King Uzziah died, I saw the Lord sitting on a throne, high and lofty; and the hem of his robe filled the temple. Seraphs were in attendance above him; each had six wings: with two they covered their faces, and with two they covered their feet, and with two they flew. And one called to another and said: "Holy, holy, holy is the Lord of hosts; the whole earth is full of his glory."

The pivots on the thresholds shook at the voices of those who called, and the house filled with smoke. And I said: "Woe is me! I am lost, for I am a man of unclean lips, and I live among a people of unclean lips; yet my eyes have seen the King, the Lord of hosts!"

Then one of the seraphs flew to me, holding a live coal that had been taken from the altar with a pair of tongs. The seraph touched my mouth with it and said, "Now that this has touched your lips, your guilt has departed and your sin is blotted out." Then I heard the voice of the Lord saying, "Whom shall I send, and who will go for us?" And I said, "Here am I; send me!"

ISAIAH 6:1–8

Some people volunteer for everything. They seem to have a nervous twitch that sends their hands into the air frequently. However, most of us think long and hard about taking on a new project. We weigh the additional responsibility, the risks, and our loss of personal time against how obligated we feel to accept or agree. What finally tips the balance from "No, not this time" to "Let me think about it" to "Send me"?

The passage above, clearly a fantasy, is one answer. Overwhelmed by a full vision of the glory of God and God's creation, the prophet becomes instantly aware of his shortcomings. He knows that he is a man of "unclean lips," that he is a mere human being and not worthy of all that has been given to him. No one wants to accomplish anything when feeling that unworthy. But an angel touches the prophet's lips with a burning coal taken from the altar, telling him that his "sin is blotted out." He is immensely relieved and grateful to know that he is valued more for what he wants to be than for what he regrets. When God asks, "Who will go for us?" he responds, "Here am I; send me!"

What moves the prophet forward is that he is given another chance. We can use as many as we get. We make our share of mistakes. Some are inconsequential, but others shake our confidence so badly we want to go away and hide. Our most devastating experiences usually include discovering that we are doing the same thing wrong repeatedly. Knowing this, we feel incompetent, stupid, and even "unclean." Then our lips are touched with a coal from that life-giving altar. It may occur when someone says, "I know how you're feeling, but I want you to try again, and I have confidence that this time you will succeed." This is a life-restoring experience, and it allows us to respond, "Yes. Here I am. Send me."

We walk through life with our "game faces" on, fearing that should we ever be unmasked and discovered, the consequences would be devastating. We need to invite one another out of hiding and offer that burning coal of forgiveness and acceptance. Then we can all release enough energy to do the work we do best in this world.

And Shall Name Him Immanuel

Again the Lord spoke to Ahaz, saying, Ask a sign of the Lord your God; let it be deep as Sheol or high as heaven. But Ahaz said, I will not ask, and I will not put the Lord to the test. Then Isaiah said: "Hear then, O house of David! Is it too little for you to weary mortals, that you weary my God also? Therefore the Lord himself will give you a sign. Look, the young woman is with child and shall bear a son, and shall name him Immanuel."

ISAIAH 7:10–14

The king is troubled. He fears the people of his kingdom have become religiously lax, morally weak, and hypocritical. He fears that God's blessing will be withdrawn, and that their enemies, sensing their vulnerability, will invade and conquer them. God says, "Ask for a sign. Ask for a blessing. I'll give it to you." Ahaz responds that he couldn't trouble God for that sort of thing, and Isaiah, the prophet, responds, "Here is the sign you need: The young woman is with child and shall bear a son, and shall name him Immanuel." *Immanuel* means "God is with us."

What an incredible blessing! God is with us. God is with us even when we feel we don't deserve it. God is with us though we have forgotten how to pray. God is not just watching over us or keeping an eye out for us from on high, but God is with us now. Perhaps God also knows our fears, frustrations, and weaknesses. Perhaps God understands how much we long to be better than we are and how we sometimes grieve when we fall short. Perhaps God is also with us when we are angry or feeling abandoned. If we believe that God is with us even when our fear of failure threatens to paralyze us, then perhaps we can act anyway.

Though the presence of God in our lives will always be a great and compelling mystery, when we believe that presence is real, everything changes. When we truly believe God is among us, then we meet one another differently. We listen a little more carefully. We are more receptive to strangers. We allow ourselves to believe that each day and every stranger can bring new and unexpected blessings.

Quakers used to address each other as "thee" and "thou," reflecting their respect for "that of God" within each person. It is a discipline that allows them to see themselves, other people, and all else in the light of the Holy. That view changes everything.

The People Who Walked in Darkness Have Seen a Great Light

The people who walked in darkness have seen a great light; those who lived in a land of deep darkness—on them light has shined. You have multiplied the nation, you have increased its joy; they rejoice before you as with joy at the harvest, as people exult when dividing plunder. For the yoke of their burden, and the bar across their shoulders, the rod of their oppressor, you have broken as on the day of Midian. . . . For a child has been born for us, a son given to us; authority rests upon his shoulders; and he is named Wonderful Counselor, Mighty God, Everlasting Father, Prince of Peace.

ISAIAH 9:2–4, 6

Imagine walking in deep darkness. If the electricity fails on a stormy night, and all the lights in your neighborhood go out, you are plunged into a disorienting blackness without any orienting light.

You can't see anything. Even in familiar places you cannot locate the sharp edges of furniture or lamps that might be knocked over. You can't see stairs. You can't see to find a flashlight or a candle. You are completely lost. In the same way, if you walk into the deep woods late at night without a flashlight, the darkness that at first seems romantic quickly becomes oppressive as you realize you are helpless to protect yourself or to find your way home.

When the Bible extols light over darkness, what is at issue is not a color preference. It is a preference for sight over helplessness. The people who live "in a land of deep darkness" are helpless to protect themselves, to avoid the sharp edges around them, and to stop knocking things over. They cannot save themselves from falling into dangerous situations. They cannot find their way home. We often speak about the "dark" moments in our own lives, and it is precisely that desperate darkness that is implied here.

When we live in deepest darkness, we live without hope, and often it is a dilemma that we help to make. We may compromise our values so that we no longer remember what it felt like to live them. Somewhere in that darkness, we lose dreams and goals that once were important. We forget where we were going and why. Friendships are broken. And sometimes we step forward without realizing how great a fall we are about to take. Our friends begin to leave us, because most people cannot bear the pain of watching their friends live in darkness.

But the passage assures us that people who walk in darkness, even in deepest darkness, will find a light to lead them out. We know this because creation's light is always seeking a way into our lives even in something as unassuming as the presence of a child. No one who retains even a shred of faith in life's power to heal and strengthen us is ever completely lost to confusion or despair for there's no darkness so deep that we cannot see a light beyond it if we are patient and hopeful. We know it as well, because past generations have left us with testimonies that in their darkest hours they found a hidden strength from an unexpected source.

Those Who Wait for the Lord

Have you not known? Have you not heard?
The Lord is the everlasting God,
    the Creator of the ends of the earth.
He does not faint or grow weary;
    his understanding is unsearchable.
He gives power to the faint,
    and strengthens the powerless.
Even youths will faint and be weary,
    and the young will fall exhausted;
but those who wait for the Lord shall renew their strength,
    they shall mount up with wings like eagles,
they shall run and not be weary,
    they shall walk and not faint.

ISAIAH 40:28–31

Our culture doesn't encourage waiting. We try to eliminate delays as much as possible and don't give ourselves much opportunity to practice patience. This passage seems to understand our impatience, because it points out that even the youth, whose energy, quickness, and enthusiasm we admire (and wish we still had) "will faint and be weary, and the young will fall exhausted." In other words, even those who are in the prime of their physical life and mental agility will have to wait for what can happen only in the fullness or in the completeness of time.

I can remember when, as a young minister, I felt desperately responsible for "saving" a troubled family or marriage or congregation. I believed that if I attended the right workshops, read the right books, and applied the correct technique, a solution would emerge and everyone would be grateful. It so often happened, however, that what my parishioners wanted was not a solution or an insight from someone else, but support for living in the tension until they could find their own way out of it. Or perhaps they were looking for the strength to stay in a relationship which, though not ideal, still gave them far more comfort and would stand the test of time better than an outsider could understand. There are meanings that come to us only when we stop trying so hard to snare them. Sometimes, those who are willing to wait "shall renew their strength" through that waiting.

Think of trying to remember the name of someone you meet on the street. This person knows a lot about you. You fake a conversation while desperately searching for the right name and connection. It doesn't work. Nothing comes to you. The conversation ends, on good terms you hope, and you both walk away. Still nothing comes. At some point you say, "I give up. I'm not going to get that information now." Minutes later, the name and connection walk into your life as innocently as if they had never known they had been missed.

Sometimes we achieve what we struggle very hard for, and these are the success stories we all treasure. But many other situations cannot and will not be resolved satisfactorily until the pressure to resolve them is off and until the time is right. Those who are willing to wait for that resolution, to "wait for the Lord," may be strengthened in the fullness of time.

I Am About to Do a New Thing

Do not remember the former things,
    or consider the things of old.
I am about to do a new thing;
    now it springs forth, do you not perceive it?
I will make a way in the wilderness
    and rivers in the desert.
The wild animals will honor me,
    the jackals and the ostriches;
for I give water in the wilderness,
    rivers in the desert,
to give drink to my chosen people,
    the people whom I formed for myself
so that they might declare my praise.

ISAIAH 43:18–21

"Do not remember the former things, or consider the things of old." There are actually many things "of old" that we are glad to remember. There is the love that has always been there for us no matter how difficult we became. There are gifts we have been given far beyond our deserving of them. Some people have stood by us in tough times and some have made the good things in our lives possible. We should remember them.

There are also painful memories we need to keep: the hurtful things we have said or done that we are determined not to repeat; those moments when courage or candor failed us and we were not the people we wanted to be. We must continue to be taught by these painful learning experiences.

Other memories poison our lives. Hurts inflicted upon us long ago still linger. We remember old humiliations, rivalries, and betrayals. We fear they will come back to bite us again, and that fear gives them power over us. Other memories anchor us in places from which we cannot grow. We don't want our lives, our friends, our children, our institutions, or our ideas to change, because we fear that change in ourselves.

"I am about to do a new thing," says God through Isaiah. If God can do a new thing, so can we. Poisonous or anchoring memories need not direct our lives. Perhaps God will do a new thing through us, something so drastic it will find a new path through the wilderness or water our own desert places. We don't know what that new thing would look like. It might be something as subtle and exciting as a new stage in our life and growth.

We have some choice about how our lives will unfold. On the one hand, we can think of ourselves as wind-up toys. Wound up in our "prime," we then walk in circles with decreasing energy as our body runs down to a stop. On the other hand, we can follow our passions and trust our intuition, which express our life and values more accurately. Learning to do a new thing at any stage of life is more than just being "outrageous," though that is how some will see it. We can recognize that God or life is never quite through bringing into being something new—even through us.

Into the Wilderness

Then Jesus was led up by the Spirit into the wilderness to be tempted by the devil. He fasted forty days and forty nights, and afterwards he was famished. The tempter came and said to him, "If you are the Son of God, command these stones to become loaves of bread." But he answered, "It is written, 'One does not live by bread alone, but by every word that comes from the mouth of God.'"

Then the devil took him to the holy city and placed him on the pinnacle of the temple, saying to him, "If you are the Son of God, throw yourself down; for it is written, 'He will command his angels concerning you,' and 'On their hands they will bear you up, so that you will not dash your foot against a stone.'" Jesus said to him, "Again it is written, 'Do not put the Lord your God to the test.'"

Again, the devil took him to a very high mountain and showed him all the kingdoms of the world and their splendor; and he said to him, "All these I will give you, if you will fall down and worship me." Jesus said to him, "Away with you, Satan! for it is written, 'Worship the Lord your God, and serve only him.'" Then the devil left him and suddenly angels came and waited on him.

MATTHEW 4:1–11

Jesus was baptized in the Jordan River. In that instant, the heavens opened and he heard God accepting him as "my Son, the Beloved, with whom I am well pleased." It would have been a moment to savor, but Jesus was immediately "led by the Spirit" into the wilderness to be tested. Apparently there was some reason why Jesus needed to live out his calling immediately, rather than wait around to enjoy his moment of blessing.

Life is full of tests, it seems, and they often come at inopportune times. When we were children, we thought we would outgrow the need for exams, but the challenges to our sensitivity and courage just keep coming. Unlike childhood's tests, adult tests are unscheduled. There isn't much time to prepare, and preparation wouldn't help anyway, because the most significant tests throw us back on our most fundamental resources. They illumine who we are. That was precisely why Jesus was led on a wilderness journey immediately after he was "ordained" by God.

He needed to find out who he was and where his strength came from, for the temptations he found in the wilderness were fairly attractive. He was starving: He could be given food. He was powerless: He could draw on the power of God. He was poor: He could become wealthy. To get out of this predicament all he needed to do was to give away his soul—his integrity, his independent judgment, his relationship to God. Comfort and security are very important to most of us, so the sacrifice of some principle or other can seem like a small price to pay to get us out of a jam. We never know what we will sacrifice or what we will hold on to until we are tested. That is why the wilderness journey is important in nearly every religious tradition.

When we begin a real mountain or desert wilderness trip, guidelines are critical to the outcome. The success of the journey will rest on everyone's effort, so we must value and trust our companions in a way that we don't normally trust most people. Honesty and compassion are critical in this. We give up some of our natural reserve and privacy to become part of the group.

Because our foremost responsibility to ourselves and others is to stay involved in the work of the group, we must also discover our own abilities to keep going even against challenges that seem impossible to meet. We give up the luxury of complaining and walking away from the job at hand. We must become good friends with whatever it is that keeps us moving forward physically one step at a time. Because depression is a luxury we cannot afford in the wilderness, we must reach out to whatever strengthens our spirit and cultivate it as the sign of a vital spiritual resource.

In any wilderness of the landscape, of the mind, or of the spirit, these qualities are important. We must value others for what they do best. We must give up personal advantages for the sake of the group. We must trust our own ability to go on even in the midst of uncertainty. We must be able to find beauty and light that will break through the gloom of our fatigue, our depression, even our despair. Perhaps sacrificing our pride, privacy, and personal advantage is a way of finding God. Clearly it was important for Jesus.

Blessed Are the Poor in Spirit

When Jesus saw the crowds, he went up the mountain; and after he sat down, his disciples came to him. Then he began to speak, and taught them, saying:

"Blessed are the poor in spirit, for theirs is the kingdom of heaven.
"Blessed are those who mourn, for they will be comforted.
"Blessed are the meek, for they will inherit the earth.
"Blessed are those who hunger and thirst for righteousness, for they will be filled.
"Blessed are the merciful, for they will receive mercy.
"Blessed are the pure in heart, for they will see God."

MATTHEW 5:1–8

Pride can be wonderful. We want our children to be proud of what they do well: It is one of our strongest wishes for them. We want to be proud of the congregations or organizations to which we belong, and we love to root for a team that is proud of itself. Therefore, when, in these opening verses of the Sermon on the Mount, Jesus bestows blessings on the "poor in spirit" and upon the "meek," his words endorse qualities we don't usually appreciate, qualities that belong to "losers" in our competitive society.

Pride can be an awful thing. There is a false pride that masks defensiveness. In its thrall, we fill up with our own importance. We cannot hear what others say to us unless it is a compliment. We cannot entertain thoughts we have not already thought. We particularly cannot see that our view of the world, a view with our self at the center of it, is shaky and distorted. There is no room in our minds or hearts for what we do not want to understand.

It is against this second notion of pride that Jesus tells his disciples, "Blessed are the poor in spirit, for theirs is the kingdom of heaven." In many versions of this passage, Jesus says to those who have given up everything to follow him, "Blessed are you, poor . . . for yours is the kingdom of heaven." The "poor" to whom he refers have not buttressed their self importance with the haughty and defensive attitude that keeps everyone else out. When they pray or seek guidance, it is not to be reassured of what they already believe but to open themselves to whatever comes to them, however unexpectedly it may arrive.

In other words, we might understand the passage this way:

Blessed are those who do not conceive themselves rich already; because they know they have much to learn, there is much more they will learn. Blessed are those who allow themselves to grieve, for by working through their grief they will find a greater strength and confidence in life. Blessed are those who do not stride over the face of the earth as if they owned all of it, for they will become much more at home. Blessed are those who hunger for justice, for their efforts will eventually bear fruit, while those who never try will never have any results. Blessed are the compassionate, for life will treat them at least as kindly as they have treated others. Blessed are those who are still open to surprise, to challenge, and to love, for their openness will bring them more blessings than they ever imagined.

Be Perfect, as Your Heavenly Father Is Perfect

You have heard that it was said, "An eye for an eye and a tooth for a tooth." But I say to you, Do not resist an evildoer. But if anyone strikes you on the right cheek, turn the other also; and if anyone wants to sue you and take your coat, give your cloak as well; and if anyone forces you to go one mile, go also the second mile. Give to everyone who begs from you, and do not refuse anyone who wants to borrow from you.

You have heard that it was said, "You shall love your neighbor and hate your enemy." But I say to you, Love your enemies and pray for those who persecute you, so that you may be children of your Father in heaven; for he makes his sun rise on the evil and on the good, and sends rain on the righteous and on the unrighteous. For if you love those who love you, what reward do you have? Do not even the tax collectors do the same? And if you greet only your brothers and sisters, what more are you doing than others? Do not even the Gentiles do the same? Be perfect, therefore, as your heavenly Father is perfect.

MATTHEW 5:38–48

Be perfect? Who can be perfect but God? That is why we join congregations or read books about the Bible. We know we are not perfect. We are far from it. We might (on our best days) try to get a bit closer to what could be expected of a religious person, but the effort to become perfect seems almost too much to ask of us without some words of instruction.

That instruction is included in these words from Jesus. The conventional wisdom of that time, and ours, is represented in these words: "You have heard it said . . . Don't let anyone push you around. Guard your territory. Give back as good as you get." Our world operates on this fortress mentality. While it makes sense in a conventional way, we also know it doesn't work. In the conventional world, if you hit me, and I hit you back, we have achieved nothing more than a standoff. If you then hit me harder and I double my response, the conflict between us never really goes away until someone separates us or we become just too tired to fight.

But if I open my heart to your grievance, your hurt, your anger, it may be that we can actually find an opening to resolve our conflict. Generosity so often amazes us because we do not expect it. It gets our attention. It is disarming. Confronted with someone else's openness, we wonder, if only for a moment, if we could live that way. And perhaps for a while we do.

We understand miserliness or defensiveness. We know why people guard their prerogatives carefully. We can appreciate why some are not very trusting. At the same time, generosity helps us realize how petty and small our lives can become. A truly generous individual makes us wonder how he or she has not become as toughened by all that has hardened our hearts. There is no easy answer for that, but the question continues to haunt us.

The passage assures us that God makes the same weather for the evil and the good, for the righteous and the unrighteous. We would have thought otherwise. If God had followed our rules for living, the evil and the unrighteous would be plagued by bad luck and terrible weather for the rest of their lives, while the sun would always follow the rest of us. That's not how God operates. Generosity, not perfection, is the soul of life. That may not make the religious life any easier, but unlike perfection, we know what generosity looks like and so the religious way becomes clearer.

Even if all we do in the following year is incorporate more generosity into our lives, then we are truly on the road to spiritual growth.

No One Can Serve Two Masters

Do not store up for yourselves treasures on earth, where moth and rust consume and where thieves break in and steal; but store up for yourselves treasures in heaven, where neither moth nor rust consumes and where thieves do not break in and steal. For where your treasure is, there your heart will be also.

The eye is the lamp of the body. So, if your eye is healthy, your whole body will be full of light; but if your eye is unhealthy, your whole body will be full of darkness. If then the light in you is darkness, how great is the darkness!

No one can serve two masters; for a slave will either hate the one and love the other, or be devoted to the one and despise the other. You cannot serve God and wealth.

Therefore I tell you, do not worry about your life, what you will eat or what you will drink, or about your body, what you will wear. Is not life more than food, and the body more than clothing? Look at the birds of the air; they neither sow nor reap nor gather into barns, and yet your heavenly Father feeds them. Are you not of more value than they? And can you by worrying add a single hour to your span of life?

MATTHEW 6:19–27

Serving two masters is exactly what we try to do when we talk about "balancing career and family" as if each were of equal weight. Consider the tension when a third master is added: a hobby like golf or an avocation like painting or writing. Add a fourth master like food, tobacco, or alcohol and we are veritably strung out among masters to placate. The words from Jesus in this passage speak to one of the central spiritual dilemmas of the first years of this century. In a world where so much is possible technologically, we are tempted to think we can have our way with any number of masters.

We are usually unaware of thinking this way. When two masters (work and home) start making demands of us at the same time, often followed by a third master (alcohol or hobby or an illicit relationship), then each master suggests that if it had our full attention, the other problems would go away. We convince ourselves we are canny enough to play one master off against another, keeping each at bay and satisfying all, but this game cannot go on for long without resolving itself at our expense. A "slave" will usually end up loving one master and hating all the others. (If alcohol is in the picture, it often wins.) A free person recognizes that multiple masters cannot always be equally served and makes choices accordingly.

Sometimes it takes a news flash to remind us that our priorities have become skewed. We learn that a wind, flood, or fire has destroyed a family's home and possessions, but the family is safe. When interviewed, the family says, "At least we are all alive, and we have each other. That's what's most important."

We wonder if we would respond as calmly in the same situation. If we lost all our furniture, clothing, appliances, "toys," and keepsakes we might not be so calm. We are forced to consider what holds our lives together, and what does not.

Jesus reminds us of God's incredible generosity and points out that, of all God's creatures, people are the only ones who worry about whether God has been generous enough. He asks, Why worry, about things, about advancement, about material reward, or the lack of it? Worrying won't add even an hour to our lives. We can and need to make choices between greater and lesser goods, between what sustains us at our best and what does not. We must learn to force ourselves to make those choices so that we can look back at where our priorities have been without regret.

Do Not Judge

Do not judge, so that you may not be judged. For with the judgment you make you will be judged, and the measure you give will be the measure you get. Why do you see the speck in your neighbor's eye, but do not notice the log in your own eye? Or how can you say to your neighbor, "Let me take the speck out of your eye," while the log is in your own eye? You hypocrite, first take the log out of your own eye, and then you will see clearly to take the speck out of your neighbor's eye. . . .

Ask, and it will be given to you; search, and you will find; knock, and the door will be opened for you. For everyone who asks receives, and everyone who searches finds, and for everyone who knocks, the door will be opened. Is there anyone among you who, if your child asks for bread, will give a stone?

MATTHEW 7:1–5, 7–9

We judge all the time. We judge the people we work with. We judge the people who serve us. We judge people on the street, and sometimes we judge our friends and family. These words from Jesus comprise one of the most troublesome passages in the Christian scriptures, because most of us cannot imagine living without making critical observations and even judgments.

Jesus does not refer to critical comments we might make to clarify our feelings, to express disagreement or irritation, or even to suggest that our patience is running out. ("I wish you would let me finish a sentence." "I think that might be the wrong tie to go with that shirt." "Perhaps you could be a little more patient with your mother.") Instead, this passage refers to judgments: hard, lasting, unalterable impressions we form and hold of one another.

Of course, we can express our anger. When we do, we usually calm down and back out of that mood. We manage to repair the relationship. By contrast, judging others is a cold, stubborn, unyielding attitude in which we establish ourselves as if we had the power and knowledge that belongs only to God. Even God avoids making final judgments, always leaving open the possibility that people can change their ways.

Those who often make hard and final judgments have very few friends, because those friends will always wonder when they will be accused of having done wrong. Instinctively, we know that an unforgiving person has a log in his or her own eye that makes it difficult to see the world as it is and to appreciate people as they really are.

Having established what we all know about judgmental people and how we react to them, the passage goes on, "Ask, and it will be given to you; search, and you will find; knock, and the door will be opened for you. For everyone who asks receives, and everyone who searches finds, and for everyone who knocks, the door will be opened. . . ." People who judge harshly see the world as tough and unyielding. They figure the world has a limited amount of goodness to give them so they'd better be first in line for the benefits. They had better make sure that those who are less worthy do not get ahead of them.

Jesus understands the world differently. He sees a bountiful world where there is beauty and grace enough for everyone who is open to it. We don't need to scrap with one another. We don't need to rate one another or to worry about where we rank among peers. Our discipline for living will include receiving thankfully what is freely given: the love that is manifest in sunsets and forests, seas and gardens, and most importantly in the hearts of others. Irritations will come and go, and they will not do us much harm, as long as we keep the people around us in our hearts and wish them as much happiness as we hope for ourselves.

Ask and it shall be given to you. Seek and you shall find. Knock and the door shall be opened.

Do to Others as You Would Have Them Do to You

In everything do to others as you would have them do to you; for this is the law and the prophets.

Enter through the narrow gate; for the gate is wide and the road is easy that leads to destruction, and there are many who take it. For the gate is narrow and the road is hard that leads to life, and there are few who find it.

Beware of false prophets, who come to you in sheep's clothing but inwardly are ravenous wolves. You will know them by their fruits. Are grapes gathered from thorns, or figs from thistles? In the same way, every good tree bears good fruit, but the bad tree bears bad fruit. A good tree cannot bear bad fruit, nor can a bad tree bear good fruit. Every tree that does not bear good fruit is cut down and thrown into the fire. Thus you will know them by their fruits.

MATTHEW 7:12–20

Jesus' first sentence here is universally known as the Golden Rule. Many who may not subscribe to much else about Christianity do say they believe in the Golden Rule. They intend to treat other people in ways they would accept being treated themselves. ("I wouldn't be upset if someone did that to me!") It's not that easy. The teaching requires greater self honesty and then living more deliberately. It asks how we would prefer to be treated by others, not just whether we would find certain actions toward us acceptable.

I once worked for a man who opened a staff meeting by saying, "I want each of you to tell me how you would prefer to be treated by the rest of us." No one knew quite what to say since the bottom line for all of us was that we wanted to keep our jobs. Silence ensued. Eventually, he answered his own question, "I'll go first. I like to be complimented lavishly."

Suddenly I realized what he was getting at. He often approached us with lavish (if sometimes insincere) compliments, and it was because he wanted to be complimented as well. I had not understood until then that he needed to receive from me what I enjoyed receiving from him. All too infrequently, I remember that what I require for my self esteem is what I need to give to others in every situation. It's not easy to hold onto this insight.

This matter of living deliberately is what Jesus means by entering through the *narrow gate*. This phrase has entered our speech as

"Keeping to the straight and narrow." But it means more than just following the rules. It means living in the full recognition that what nurtures us, nurtures others and we share some responsibility for nurturing others as well as ourselves. The Golden Rule actually requires much self searching and a sincere commitment to live as if other people were as important as ourselves.

Finally, "beware of false prophets." Stay away from anyone who thinks that leading a moral life is easy, that it will lead to easy gain, that merely giving verbal assent to certain ideas will bring goodness magically into our lives. In reality, it requires a complete reorientation of our lives.

Great Is Your Faith

Jesus left that place and went away to the district of Tyre and Sidon. Just then a Canaanite woman from that region came out and started shouting, "Have mercy on me, Lord, Son of David; my daughter is tormented by a demon." But he did not answer her at all. And his disciples came and urged him, saying, "Send her away, for she keeps shouting after us." He answered, "I was sent only to the lost sheep of the house of Israel." But she came and knelt before him, saying "Lord, help me." He answered, "It is not fair to take the children's food and throw it to the dogs." She said, "Yes, Lord, yet even the dogs eat the crumbs that fall from their masters' table." Then Jesus answered her, "Woman, great is your faith! Let it be done for you as you wish." And her daughter was healed instantly.

MATTHEW 15:21–28

We're going to treat this story as a parable. This means it leaves open more questions than it answers, and the facts in the story are not as important as the questions it asks. The story is a little shocking. Jesus is approached by a woman, who is clearly not Jewish. She wants him to heal her daughter. Initially, Jesus rejects her gently, telling her he is a Jewish healer and not available to Gentiles, and then he rejects her brutally comparing her to dogs that lurk around waiting for table scraps. The woman comes right back to him, still believing that he can be reached, that his compassion can be engaged. She's right. Jesus finally answers her, "Woman, great is your faith" and tells her that her daughter will be healed.

In most of the scriptures, Jesus is the soul of patience and under-standing. Not here. Here, he responds as any of us would. He is tired. Someone he doesn't know is shouting to get his attention. His disciples are saying, "Oh, please, Master, send her away. Haven't you done enough?" Jesus responds out of that same irritable mood. The woman could have reacted in the same way and gone away angry. Instead she spoke out of her own faith. Whether it was a faith that Jesus was a better person than he seemed or a faith that something would be done to cure her daughter or a faith that she had the neces-sary powers of persuasion is just not clear. It doesn't need to be.

Let us give thanks for those who don't give up on us. They can be very irritating, because they nag a lot. They do not easily accept our explanations for our bad decisions or behavior and sometimes they confront us with the distance between what we say we believe and how we behave. We need people like that in our lives.

Let us give thanks to those who are devoted to their cause. Sometimes they are wrong, or they become so uncompromising that they do more harm than good. But they remind us—and we always need this reminder—that some things in this world are worth fighting for.

Finally, let us give thanks for those who believe in themselves. They may be incredibly misguided, but their confidence in themselves can be energizing for everyone around them.

When we say we have faith, we do not mean that we accept certain specific beliefs. We mean that we give our best and fullest energies to the hope that something good will happen. Those energies flow into the sea of whatever is healing and positive, making that force stronger and more difficult to resist. Let us give thanks for all of the tributaries that flow into that sea.

How Can One Feed These People with Bread?

In those days when there was again a great crowd without anything to eat, he called his disciples and said to them, "I have compassion for the crowd, because they have been with me now for three days and have nothing to eat. If I send them away hungry to their homes, they will faint on the way—and some of them have come from a great distance." His disciples replied, "How can one feed these people with bread here in the desert?" He asked them, "How many loaves do you have?" They said, "Seven." Then he ordered the crowd to sit down on the ground; and he took the seven loaves, and after giving thanks he broke them and gave them to his disciples to distribute; and they distributed them to the crowd. They had also a few small fish; and after blessing them, he ordered that these too should be distributed. They ate and were filled; and they took up the broken pieces left over, seven baskets full. Now

there were about four thousand people. And he sent
them away.

MARK 8:1–9

If the casseroles seem to be coming in slowly at any church supper, someone is sure to joke with the minister, asking if he or she has any "loaves and fishes" magic to increase the amount of food on the table. It's a common assumption that Jesus magically multiplied the loaves and fishes in this story, but if we look carefully it does not say that he did. The passage only says, "They ate and were filled." It also suggests that there was food left over after about "four thousand people" partook. If we understand this as a factual account, it seems nearly impossible that four thousand people were satisfied with the substance of seven loaves of bread and "a few small fish." It is not factual, of course, and the key to the passage is "They ate and were filled."

Jesus had been with these people for three days. He had not invited them to hang around and had no obligation to feed them. They must have known the disciples had brought only enough for themselves, and they probably didn't expect to be fed from that supply. But Jesus recognized their hunger. He knew they had come from some distance and felt compassion for them. So he asked them to sit down on the ground, reflecting that he took them seriously and was inviting them to share a meal with him. He said a prayer, including them in the blessing of the meal. Then he instructed his disciples to distribute the meal personally. They ate and were filled, not because their sides were bursting, but because their hunger had been met in the most important way possible. They had been encountered and cared for. They felt they had been known by someone who mattered to them.

Have you ever been in this situation? You are invited to a dinner that a friend has offered to cook. You are really looking forward to it, because of how much you value the friendship. But your host spends most of the evening hopping up and down, cooking and serving, and then worrying about the meal as if his performance as chef is more important to him than his reception of you as a friend. The food cooked may or may not have been a success, and it may or may not have been plentiful, but the evening was not what you hoped for. Very possibly you did not feel filled, because what you had hoped for in friendship was not present at that time.

There is real hunger, no question about that. This passage, however, speaks of our hunger for meaning, purpose, and companionship in a lonely world. It suggests that our deepest pangs are not satisfied by what comes out of the kitchen, but by what passes between friends because of their commitment to a true relationship.

Do Not Be Afraid

In that region there were shepherds living in the fields, keeping watch over their flock by night. Then an angel of the Lord stood before them, and then the glory of the Lord shone around them, and they were terrified. But the angel said to them, "Do not be afraid; for see—I am bringing you good news of great joy for all the people: to you is born this day in the city of David a Savior, who is the Messiah, the Lord. This will be a sign for you: you will find a child wrapped in bands of cloth and lying in a manger." And suddenly there was with the angel a multitude of the heavenly host, praising God and saying, "Glory to God in the highest heaven, and on earth peace among those whom he favors!"

LUKE 2:8–14

The fear of the shepherds seems like a perfectly reasonable response. They are camped on a hillside, half asleep, half awake for sounds of restlessness among the sheep or the howl of a predator. Suddenly an angel appears, accompanied by who knows what fanfare, which alone would have scattered the sheep. It is likely the shepherds were not accustomed to being visited by angels. How could they have known whether this angel was the "real thing" or an evil apparition? They had no reason to believe the good news that a savior would be found lying in a stable. In that moment they had many reasons to be afraid.

Then and now, there are plenty of things to fear. There are people who would cheat or harm us. There are tragedies brought about by just a moment's inattention. Economic insecurities intrude into most people's lives. Everyone fears for their health at one point or another. Sooner or later, death awaits us all. The great challenge of living well is to balance those fears so that they do not consume our waking moments. "Do not be afraid" is a tall order for any of us.

What is remarkable about this story is the calmness we feel when we read it, making the angel's command seem perfectly reasonable. Many love this passage, and the story surrounding it, precisely because, once a year for a moment or two, it brings peacefulness into their lives. Some manage to extend the calm into the rest of their living.

Perhaps we suspect that the same angel has been present to us as well, offering us the message "Trust yourself" or "Give it a chance" or "You can do this thing that scares you so much." Receiving this message is always a mixed blessing. It frightens us because usually we are asked to take a chance or make a journey to some place we've never been and may be afraid to enter. Those who take the risk and go often discover it was the right decision and appreciate the push that got them going.

Be not afraid. Really? Sure, there are some circumstances to be feared but not nearly as many as we daily imagine. It helps to remember that.

Mary Treasured All These Words and Pondered Them in Her Heart

When the angels had left them and gone into heaven, the shepherds said to one another, "Let us go now to Bethlehem and see this thing that has taken place, which the Lord has made known to us." So they went with haste and found Mary and Joseph, and the child lying in the manger. When they saw this, they made known what had been told them about this child; and all who heard it were amazed at what the shepherds told them. But Mary treasured all these words and pondered them in her heart.

LUKE 2:15–19

Whatever Mary is thinking she keeps it to herself. All of the others who hear the angel are "amazed." They babble on excitedly about this incredible occurrence, this wonderful child, this favored one of God, but Mary is silent—and thus reminds us of some of the most private thoughts of all new parents.

"What an incredible miracle is this squirming, smiling little being that is come into my life. Will I have the strength and the patience to raise this child? How can I be responsible for guiding this young life? If I have been just barely wise enough to achieve some of my own goals, how can I be wise enough to help her achieve hers? If I have had barely enough love for myself, how can I love her enough to support her through the trials of growing up? Can I always protect her? What if one day I cannot? On the other hand, I know I can never protect her completely. I should not protect her from every challenge. How will I know when to keep her safe and when to let her go and how will I bear the pain of watching her go away, as some day she must?"

We are allowed to get closer to Mary in this passage than we ever get to most of the figures in the Bible, including her son. And this may be why some religious traditions almost worship Mary.

But the passage also tells us something about ourselves and, more importantly, about others. Everyone is laden with the hopes, dreams, and fears of their parents. Even people we dislike! This should give us pause. Everyone was once a child of promise and is still a child of God. When we understand this, even if for only a moment, then for that moment we learn to look at one another very differently. In the moment in which Mary ponders her sacred responsibilities, she reminds us that every child is a repository of special hopes and dreams.

It Is to Such as These that the Kingdom of God Belongs

People were bringing even infants to him that he might touch them; and when the disciples saw it, they sternly ordered them not to do it. But Jesus called for them and said, "Let the little children come to me, and do not stop them; for it is to such as these that the kingdom of God belongs. Truly I tell you, whoever does not receive the kingdom of God as a little child will never enter it."

LUKE 18:15–17

The King James translation of this passage suggests that Jesus said, "Suffer little children to come unto me" or, as many heard it, "Let the little children suffer to come unto me." It was not a great promotion for children's religious education. However, as the above translation shows, the passage means something else entirely. The disciples were annoyed that people brought their infants for Jesus to bless. They saw this as a distraction to their work and tried to prevent it.

But Jesus intervened and told them, "It is to such as these that the kingdom of God belongs."

What does he mean by the kingdom of God? Scholars debate whether that kingdom is a present or future time; whether it is a kingdom to be established in this world or in another and what the entry requirements might be. We will not dwell on those questions. Let it suffice that the "kingdom of God" is the most wonderful state of existence we can imagine.

How do we get there? According to some, Jesus taught that we should become as little children, which seems to equate Christianity with a kind of childish faith. Most of us cannot go back to viewing the world with a child's conviction that parents, teachers, and pastors know everything and the world is a dreamy place where all good things are possible. Did Jesus really intend for his disciples to unlearn everything their lives had taught them?

Looking more closely, Jesus said, "Whoever does not *receive* the kingdom of God as a little child will never enter it." Little children, particularly infants, *receive* the world with wonder and curiosity. They are excited to learn. They take nothing for granted. They laugh easily because they find everything so funny. They do not yet make social distinctions. They do not yet worry about whether they are better or worse off than others. They do not yet require a fortress of personal possessions to serve as their symbols of power.

We are kept from the kingdom of God by our inability to receive the world as the bountiful blessing that it is. We no longer recognize that our lives are given out of God's love and are fully sufficient for our happiness. Instead, we look for distinctions of pride and place to shore up our fragile dignity and prestige. Jesus does not want us to be like children after we have become adults. Jesus wants us to receive the sunrise and the sunset, the apple and the pear, the hand and the foot, and those who would care for us as the miracles they are—as reflections of the love in which we are always held.

Why Do You Look for the Living Among the Dead?

But on the first day of the week, at early dawn, they came to the tomb, taking the spices that they had prepared. They found the stone rolled away from the tomb, but when they went in, they did not find the body. While they were perplexed about this, suddenly two men in dazzling clothes stood beside them. The women were terrified and bowed their faces to the ground, but the men said to them, "Why do you look for the living among the dead? He is not here, but has risen."

LUKE 24:1–5

There have been several times during my ministries when I have been present at or shortly after the death of a parishioner. The thought of it scared me at first, as it does many people. My experiences, however, confirmed every time that, when we die, all that we are, our "spirit," departs the body we leave behind. We then treat the body respectfully and put it to rest, knowing that what we knew and loved about this person no longer needs it.

I don't know where those we love reside after they leave us, but I do know where they can be experienced. They can be found in gatherings of their family and friends as a presence so palpable that people sometimes remark on feeling it there. This is why the traditional wake is often a very therapeutic experience.

They can be found, sometimes, in the dreams of those left behind. They are so powerfully present in our waking thoughts and actions that we imagine they are still with us in some way. Sometimes we imagine we are them.

Clearly, the dead who have made a profound impact upon us are never dead to us. We do not leave them in cemeteries. We take them with us, and though death changes our relationship, our ties to important people we have lost are never severed and never cease to be influential. We will often find our loved ones among the living in many palpable ways.

This passage reflects the experience of Jesus' disciples following his death. They returned to the tomb, expecting to prepare his body for final burial, and they found the tomb empty. And then they were asked, "Why do you look for the living among the dead?" This question, better than any other, reflects the experience of the first Christians who struggled to understand an unseen but unmistakable presence which continued to hold them together. Is it resurrection or loving memory or something else that bonds us with those who have shaped our lives in important ways? We'll never know in this world. We just have to welcome it, and that will be enough.

And the Darkness Did
Not Overcome It

In the beginning was the Word, and the Word was with
God, and the Word was God. He was in the beginning
with God. All things came into being through him,
and without him not one thing came into being. What
has come into being in him was life, and the life was
the light of all people. The light shines in the darkness,
and the darkness did not overcome it.

JOHN 1:1–5

This passage contains the essential affirmation of the Judaic and
Christian traditions that God has intended for things to work out
well for us. God has offered to us a beacon of God's goodness and
wisdom, which shall be a light shining against the darkness, a light
the darkness cannot extinguish. For many Christians, and for the
author of this passage, that light is the life and resurrection of Jesus
of Nazareth.

Since the darkness in human affairs can be a formidable adversary, this affirmation seems an extraordinary leap of faith. We need look no further than the mass slaughter of innocents that occurs somewhere in the world every year. We see the darkness in economic and political systems that grind people down while faulting them for becoming victims. We see it in the entrenched racism practiced by people all over the world. We see it in our own neglect of those whose lives we could make easier but do not. It does sometimes seem the darkness has pretty nearly taken over.

Keeping faith that something is more powerful than violence has been the great task of Western religion. Against the accumulation of our callousness and injustice, many have speculated that the gospel writers and the Jewish prophets may have been whistling in the dark, leaving the rest of us to make the best of a bad situation.

Trying to find that word of hope in the early twentieth century, Albert Schweitzer attempted to discover whether Jesus' message of love could be traced to the real, historical Jesus. He did not find the assurances he hoped for, but his conclusion was quite out of keeping with the pessimism of his time. He concluded that when we begin to walk in Jesus' footsteps, living as best we can the life he would have lived, then we will soon learn that he is real.

How do we know there is a light shining for hope and kindness and that the darkness will not extinguish it? We commit ourselves to push back the bleakness in our own lives and the darkness around us. We give ourselves to a life that is generous, compassionate, and caring despite our doubts that it will accomplish anything. As we struggle against the cynicism of the world, we will know soon enough that the light really is there and the darkness cannot finally prevail.

As the Spirit Gave Them Ability

When the day of Pentecost had come, they were all together in one place. And suddenly from heaven there came a sound like the rush of a violent wind, and it filled the entire house where they were sitting. Divided tongues, as of fire, appeared among them, and a tongue rested on each of them. All of them were filled with the Holy Spirit and began to speak in other languages, as the Spirit gave them ability.

Now there were devout Jews from every nation under heaven living in Jerusalem. And at this sound the crowd gathered and was bewildered, because each one heard them speaking in the native language of each. Amazed and astonished, they asked, "Are not all these who are speaking Galileans? And how is it that we hear, each of us, in our own native language? Parthians, Medes, Elamites, and residents of Meso-potamia, Judea, and Cappadocia, Pontus and Asia,

Phrygia and Pamphylia, Egypt and the parts of Libya belonging to Cyrene, and visitors from Rome, both Jews and proselytes, Cretans and Arabs—in our own languages we hear them speaking about God's deeds of power." All were amazed and perplexed, saying to one another, "What does this mean?" But others sneered and said, "They are filled with new wine."

ACTS 2:1–13

A little history is in order here. After Jesus' death, his disciples' first inclination was to run away so they would not be arrested. But something, a power, an attraction they hadn't expected drew them back together. Meeting again in Jerusalem, they resealed the bond they had forged with one another through common meals with Jesus. Through their sharing, they knew he had not abandoned them. What they had invested together had not been foolish or in vain. Something of Jesus was with them still. It was a presence they could neither describe adequately nor deny.

Eventually each disciple told the others what happened in his or her relationship with their friend and leader. Speaking to one another and telling the story of what happened to them was so important, so intense that it must have seemed as though "tongues of fire" had rested upon each of them. They struggled to describe very personal experiences and came to feel they could be understood by each other only "as the Spirit gave them ability." They were so on fire with new hope that outsiders who watched them concluded they must have been drunk on new wine.

I am struck by how many people have said to me, "You're the only one who might believe that this happened to me." What they then relate is a vitally important, intimate, and personal experience that has made an incredible difference in their lives. Because it was intimate, it was difficult to express in conventional language, but their initial attempts to describe it caused their friends to withdraw or to react as one would to someone who is not in the full possession of their best faculties.

So much about the spiritual life is difficult to describe in conventional language. We owe it to our friends and ourselves to pay attention to a vision, dream, or a thought that comes to us in a very compelling way. Of course, it could be a delusion, but it could also be a much more powerful message.

We could all use a little more humility in the presence of what we do not completely understand.

I Do Not Do the Good I Want, but the Evil I Do Not Want Is What I Do

I do not understand my own actions. For I do not do what I want, but I do the very thing I hate. Now if I do what I do not want, I agree that the law is good. But in fact it is no longer I that do it, but sin that dwells within me. For I know that nothing good dwells within me, that is, in my flesh. I can will what is right, but I cannot do it. For I do not do the good I want, but the evil I do not want is what I do.

So I find it to be a law that when I want to do what is good, evil lies close at hand. For I delight in the law of God in my inmost self, but I see in my members another law at war with the law of my mind, making me captive to the law of sin that dwells in my members. Wretched man that I am! Who will rescue me from this body of death?

ROMANS 7:15–19, 21–24

"I do not understand my own actions." We've been there. Perhaps we thought that in some magical "maturity" we would be fully in charge of our lives. Then we would behave at all times rationally and consistently. Perhaps we thought joining a religion or practicing a philosophy would help match what we profess with what we actually do. And yet the Book of Common Prayer tells the truth of our lives in this passage from a confession that is repeated every Sunday, "We have left undone those things which we ought to have done, and we have done those things which we ought not to have done."

What we have left undone, aside from countless chores, are the many acts of caring that were so easily within our power to do: expressions of appreciation, recognitions of others' accomplishments, and chances to give away what has come so easily to us. We have also left undone standing up for those who could use our support, encouraging those who desperately need it, and defending ideals that the world too easily barters away.

What have we done that we ought not to have done? There was the cutting word, the gesture of indifference which cruelly told a friend we were not listening. There is money we spend on activities that are not good for us. There is our unkind assessment of someone, which only reflects our jealousy, and there is the story we told that never should have been repeated. It is difficult to understand why we have done and continue to do these things. It is equally difficult to understand why we have left undone those acts of kindness and courage which we usually say reflect our beliefs.

The passage equates these actions with the sins of the flesh. The Book of Common Prayer uses the more elegant, or at least more comfortable, wording, "We have followed too much the devices and desires of our own hearts." It is just not in us. It is not in most of us to achieve complete harmony among our beliefs, our values, and our actions. Utopian ideas and communities have come and gone, because no matter how noble our thoughts and intentions, something very human will stand in the way of our realizing them fully or even largely.

Here's what's important. As long as we know this about ourselves, as long as we realize how perilously close we always are to disappointing ourselves, we will come closer to realizing our best intentions. Truly good people are always aware that they can and do fail themselves. This knowledge helps them to be kind or caring when they need to be and courageous when they need to be. Folks who never question the purity or the rightness of their thoughts and motivations tend to make poor friends, poor participants, and devastating leaders.

Let us keep one another honest, and let us cherish those communities of worship or mutual support that help keep us honest.

Do Not Be Conformed to This World

I appeal to you therefore, brothers and sisters, by the mercies of God, to present your bodies as a living sacrifice, holy and acceptable to God, which is your spiritual worship. Do not be conformed to this world, but be transformed by the renewing of your minds, so that you may discern what is the will of God—what is good and acceptable and perfect. . . .

Let love be genuine; hate what is evil, hold fast to what is good; love one another with mutual affection; outdo one another in showing honor. Do not lag in zeal, be ardent in spirit, serve the Lord. Rejoice in hope, be patient in suffering, persevere in prayer. Contribute to the needs of the saints; extend hospitality to strangers.

Bless those who persecute you; bless and do not curse them. Rejoice with those who rejoice, weep with those who weep. Live in harmony with one another;

do not be haughty, but associate with the lowly; do not claim to be wiser than you are. Do not repay anyone evil for evil, but take thought for what is noble in the sight of all. If it is possible, so far as it depends on you, live peaceably with all. Beloved, never avenge yourselves, but leave room for the wrath of God; for it is written, "Vengeance is mine, I will repay, says the Lord." No, "if your enemies are hungry, feed them; if they are thirsty, give them something to drink; for by doing this you will heap burning coals on their heads." Do not overcome by evil, but overcome evil with good.

ROMANS 12:1–2, 9–21

It is difficult not to be conformed to this world. If you are ambitious, you have to conform to a certain degree. If you want your voice to be heard, you must dress so that others will take you seriously. That's conformity. If you want people to talk and work with you, you must master whatever lubricates the gears of relationships among your peers. That's conformity.

It is difficult to resist being conformed to the culture around us. It shapes the language we use, the images and concepts that express our fears, doubts, and hopes. When we are pressured, we talk about *stress*, a word our culture has elevated to the status of a symptom. We worry that our children are too *programmed*, a word that comes from the computer industry as do so many other words we rely on to express our feelings. There are nonconformists who, in many ways, separate themselves from all of these cultural influences, but I don't think that's what the passage means.

Instead, it refers to a way of dealing with people that is thoughtful, gentle, and purposeful. The culture this passage imagines and asks us to resist is what we live with today. Are there people who persecute us? Culture tells us we should take the initiative against them or at least mount a strong defense. Are there those who weep openly? Culture tells us to avoid them if they weep too much, because their weeping is embarrassing. Have we been successful? Culture tells us to flaunt it, so that others will be impressed and bring more success our way. Do we think we've been betrayed or cheated? Our culture tells us, "Don't get mad, get even."

This passage suggests that we bless those who persecute us, weep with those who are sad, and share happiness wherever possible. It suggests that we treat our enemies with kindness, try to win them over, and never resort to vengeance. This is true nonconformity, and the only kind that really matters. It asks us to think before we act. It asks us to think about the loving or considerate response we would like to receive in the same situation. By contrast, most of us, most of the time, react. We respond to situations in a way that our world has programmed into us.

We must choose how we will be in the world, knowing we are children of a divine spark, who know we are in relationship with other sons and daughters of the Holy. That choice calls for a radical reorientation of our lives.

There Are Varieties of Gifts

Now there are varieties of gifts, but the same Spirit; and there are varieties of services, but the same Lord; and there are varieties of activities, but it is the same God who activates all of them in everyone. To each is given the manifestation of the Spirit for the common good. To one is given through the Spirit the utterance of wisdom, and to another the utterance of knowledge according to the same Spirit, to another faith by the same Spirit, to another gifts of healing by the one Spirit, to another the working of miracles, to another prophecy, to another the discernment of spirits, to another various kinds of tongues, to another the interpretation of tongues. All these are activated by one and the same Spirit, who allots to each one individually just as the Spirit chooses.

1 CORINTHIANS 12:4–11

When someone else can do something better than we can, we feel a bit envious and wish we had that talent also. We may convince ourselves that if we tried hard enough—really tried—we could master that skill too, and then we would be complete. We believe that if we mastered that skill, we would have a higher opinion of ourselves, and others would have a higher opinion of us.

Introverts wish they could move as easily among crowds of people as their extrovert friends do. And extraverts wish that they had the deep centeredness that their introvert friends possess. Those who have a talent for organizing sometimes find that they can organize a group but they cannot get it to move, while those who know they can inspire a group to go forward often don't have the talent to coordinate what happens next.

The Apostle Paul wrote this passage to his congregation in Corinth, because each member of that congregation, in a struggle to be the perfect congregational leader, was getting in the way of the others. Each wanted to possess all the good qualities that generally adhere to leaders and then to crowd the others out of the light. What resulted was far from what Paul had in mind as a community drawn together in the memory of Jesus

His tells them that the Spirit does not give even the possibility that one person could have all the talents. We imagine the perfect human being is one who thinks deeply but moves well in crowds and loves being with people. This person has a good sense of organizing principles and can move us forward to do radical things. He or she is clear about the rules but can apply them with compassion and even know when the rules do not apply. These qualities do not exist in one person. Therefore, we must rely on each other. We've each been given certain gifts, but we haven't been given all of them. Our world requires that we learn to use our gifts well, trusting that the talents of others will provide the balance of all the gifts that no one, alone, can provide.

The difference in outlook here is profound. On the one hand, we know we can do some things well but recognize there are weaknesses in our skills. We feel responsible to shore up every weakness into a strength, an effort that cannot possibly succeed. On the other hand, we recognize that we have specific God-given gifts. We are responsible to learn to use those gifts well but also to recognize that the same Spirit that gave us our gifts needs us to work cooperatively with those who have different but complementary gifts. We are all extensions of the same Spirit, and not, as it so often feels, independent, complete, and competing expressions of that Spirit.

Once we know that life has touched us with special gifts—and that are ours to use well, but that we will never be given everything special—then we can cease berating ourselves and begin to live.

The Greatest of These Is Love

If I speak in the tongues of mortals and of angels, but do not have love, I am a noisy gong or a clanging cymbal. And if I have prophetic powers, and understand all mysteries and all knowledge, and if I have all faith, so as to remove mountains, but do not have love, I am nothing. If I give away all my possessions, and if I hand over my body so that I may boast, but do not have love, I gain nothing.

Love is patient; love is kind; love is not envious or boastful or arrogant or rude. It does not insist on its own way; it is not irritable or resentful; it does not rejoice in wrongdoing, but rejoices in the truth. It bears all things, believes all things, hopes all things, endures all things.

Love never ends. But as for prophecies, they will come to an end; as for tongues, they will cease; as for knowledge, it will come to an end. For we know only in part, and we prophesy only in part; but when the complete comes, the partial will come to an end. When I was a child, I spoke like a child, I thought like a child, I reasoned like a child; when I became an adult, I put an end to childish ways. For now we see in a mirror, dimly, but then we will see face to face. Now I know only in part; then I will know fully, even as I have been fully known. And now faith, hope, and love abide, these three; and the greatest of these is love.

1 CORINTHIANS 13:1–13

The congregation in Corinth was a troublesome lot. Everyone wanted to be the star of the show. Some thought they could preach up a storm better than anyone else. Others thought they were leaders, planners, or deciders, and believed their particular skills ought to move them to the head of the line. Each asserted that he or she was for the greater good of the congregation, but each also wanted to be the most "important."

In this letter, Paul says that it doesn't much matter what you do or how "important" you think you are unless you care about what happens to other people. That's what he means by "love." Can you feel the pain of the people with whom you work and does their happiness or joy or sense of security increase your own? If you cannot imagine and touch the lives of those with whom you work, whatever you accomplish may benefit you, but will help no one else and will have little value in the full scheme of things. The word love has many meanings, ranging from passionate erotic attachments to a vaguely affectionate embrace of humankind, but for Paul it means a significant engagement with the welfare of other people.

This passage should give us pause. Have we acted primarily in the service of others or have we more often intended to gain personal glory? Most of the rewards we work for as adults are like the merits we accumulated when we were kids; they once seemed important but that importance faded with time and continues to fade.

This was probably what Paul meant when he wrote, "When I was a child, I spoke like a child, I thought like a child, I reasoned like a child; when I became an adult, I put an end to childish ways. For now we see in a mirror, dimly, but then we will see face to face."

When we were young, we looked through a "mirror dimly,"—we saw only ourselves, our issues, our power, our sense of importance. At the end of our lives, "when we see face to face," we may realize we have spent our years working for incentives that promoted personal power without much concern for other people. It seems that in God's sight our happiness is intimately connected to the happiness of others. If we look carefully at the connections in our lives we see that much of what we think of as "ours" has been given to us through a complex web of relationships and love. We see our responsibility to give back some of what has nurtured us.

Be Angry but Do Not Sin

You were taught to put away your former way of life, your old self, corrupt and deluded by its lusts, and to be renewed in the spirit of your minds, and to clothe yourselves with the new self, created according to the likeness of God in true righteousness and holiness.

So then, putting away falsehood, let us all speak the truth to our neighbors, for we are members of one another. Be angry but do not sin; do not let the sun go down on your anger, and do not make room for the devil. Thieves must give up stealing; rather let them labor and work honestly with their own hands, so as to have something to share with the needy. Let no evil talk come out of your mouths, but only what is useful for building up, as there is need, so that your words may give grace to those who hear.

EPHESIANS 4:22–29

The original recipients of these words wondered what it meant to lead a Christian life. Clearly it meant, and still means, a deliberate and thoughtful break from our former lives. It meant being honest with others, for Christians enter into a communal bond that dishonesty would destroy. Apparently former thieves numbered among them, because the passage singles them out with the warning to give up stealing. It also prohibited "evil talk," which destroys relationships and communities.

When we read these passages thoughtfully we may be impressed with how it raises the bar pretty high for most of us. We wonder, "But, but, what about . . . ?" We react to the knowledge that our anger is usually what gets us into trouble. Anger is on the front or back burner for everyone. Most days bring us minor irritations, which we work hard to suppress, but there are also smoldering resentments, and some experience a deeply seated, free-floating fury so elusive it can be difficult to sort out.

Since angry people are unpleasant and often difficult to deal with, our parents and teachers have taught us to disguise our anger as something else. Rather than risk confrontation, some people engage in covert gossip or backbiting. Others find ways to make everyone around them miserable while denying that they are angry at anyone or anything. Unacknowledged rage in our relationships can destroy them more effectively than anything else.

This passage counsels those who would enter into a new way of living to "Be angry but do not sin." Everyone will get angry; to remain healthy we must express that anger. When we speak, we need to make ourselves clearly understood. We should avoid words that drip with vindictiveness or burn with a rage that often comes from an unknown source. If an apology will help, we should let others know why we feel one is due to us and be prepared to make our own.

If there is some change that would ease the tension, we need to say what that change would look like. We need to put our serious disagreements on the table or our lack of honesty will pollute our relationships and our community.

The final passage, which concerns giving "grace to those who hear," is often understood as suggesting that we say nothing that would annoy, trouble, anger, or offend another person. There are times when that would not be honest. When our angry actions belie our gentle words, we end up trailing a wake of frustrated and confused relationships. In all that we do, we must try to build trust, understanding, and healing rather than trying only to win. Let us speak thoughtfully, honestly, and with a care for those who are listening to what may be difficult to hear.

The Assurance of Things Hoped For

But recall those earlier days when, after you had been enlightened, you endured a hard struggle with sufferings, sometimes being publicly exposed to abuse and persecution, and sometimes being partners with those so treated. For you had compassion for those who were in prison, and you cheerfully accepted the plundering of your possessions, knowing that you yourselves possessed something better and more lasting. Do not, therefore, abandon that confidence of yours; it brings a great reward. For you need endurance, so that when you have done the will of God, you may receive what was promised. . . .

Now faith is the assurance of things hoped for, the conviction of things not seen. Indeed, by faith our ancestors received approval. By faith we understand that the worlds were prepared by the word of God, so that what is seen was made from things that are not visible.

HEBREWS 10:32–36, 11:1–3

The author of Hebrews is thought to be writing to a generation of Christians who believed their faith would change the world. Instead they were persecuted for that faith and became discouraged. So the leader of their community sat down to write a long rational defense of his own beliefs. In this passage, he gets to the heart of it: "Faith is the assurance of things hoped for, the conviction of things unseen."

Faith is what happens when you feel a deep certainty that what you hope for has a good chance of coming true eventually, despite all evidence to the contrary. We may hope to establish more communities founded upon compassion and justice. Since we lack proof that these communities will be created soon, the only thing left to us is faith—a deep certainty that these ideas and hopes are simply right. Therefore, they must prevail though we may live only long enough to nudge them a little further ahead. Living with that faith, perhaps seeing through its eyes, we may recognize that some such communities now exist where once they did not.

"What is seen was made from things that are not visible." We've all witnessed surprising and wonderful changes in our friends and family members, for which we had no preparation or warning. What happened then happened because of things that "are not visible." Though they were there all along, we did not see them.

How many times have you been surprised by good things you didn't expect to happen? Your children, who once didn't seem to have a serious thought in their minds, suddenly develop a firm sense of purpose and direction. Friends who had struggled to make their relationship work, mysteriously find the way that had eluded them. Individuals who did not seem courageous suddenly develop a backbone and take a stand when it is needed. Decisions that confused us suddenly become clear. Events no one could have anticipated or even understood surprise us, and they chip away at our apathy and indifference.

What we see is often made out of things that were not clear to us at first. As long as we have the capacity to believe in great things, the energy and wisdom to achieve those goals is at work in the universe, whether or not we see it working.

Strangers and Pilgrims

These all died in faith, not having received the promises, but having seen them afar off, and were persuaded of them, and embraced them, and confessed that they were strangers and pilgrims on the earth. For they that say such things declare plainly that they seek a country. And truly, if they had been mindful of that country from whence they came out, they might have had opportunity to have returned. But now they desire a better country, that is, an heavenly: wherefore God is not ashamed to be called their God: for he hath prepared for them a city.

HEBREWS 11:13–16

The men and women who settled on the southern coast of Massachusetts in 1620 knew themselves as Pilgrims because they were familiar with this passage and believed they were on a sacred quest.

They deliberately left two countries, where they could have lived comfortably enough, for a place they could not begin to imagine when they set sail. It was not going to be heaven—they were sure of that—but they were determined to make it as close to their view of heaven as they possibly could.

This passage challenges us to think about how our lives should unfold. It suggests a contrast between living a pilgrimage toward a goal that is dear to us and living an odyssey, as many people do today. If our life is an odyssey, then we may start out toward a specific goal, but our aim and desire eventually become just finding a place that is safe and comfortable. Someone on an odyssey is never quite sure where the winds will blow him or her but hopes to find enough safe harbors to make the journey worthwhile.

A pilgrimage, by contrast, is a deliberate search for a specific place, a personal goal, a station in life, a standard of religious integrity, a place that is more meaningful to us than anywhere else. A pilgrim knows the way will be difficult and that adjustments may have to be made en route, but never doubts the outcome, because it is just too important.

When we listen to friends tell their life stories, we recognize that some are caught up in daring, carefree, or reckless wanderings, which we euphemistically call "interesting lives." Others have carefully chosen to be pilgrims in the hope that reaching their goals will reward them for the costs of hewing carefully to one vision. Some start out on a pilgrimage, but abandon it and happily become wanderers. Others transform their lives by deciding to stop wandering and choose a goal that enlists their full commitment and energy.

Will your life be an odyssey or a pilgrimage? Will it have a guiding value or be open to whatever comes along? Your choice will make a big difference in how your life turns out.

Entertaining Angels
Without Knowing It

Let mutual love continue. Do not neglect to show hospitality to strangers, for by doing that some have entertained angels without knowing it. Remember those who are in prison, as though you were in prison with them; those who are being tortured, as though you yourselves were being tortured. Let marriage be held in honor by all, and let the marriage bed be kept undefiled; for God will judge fornicators and adulterers. Keep your lives free from the love of money, and be content with what you have; for he has said, "I will never leave you or forsake you." So we can say with confidence, "The Lord is my helper; I will not be afraid. What can anyone do to me?"

HEBREWS 13:1–6

In the desert world of this scripture, when a traveler appears at your home, you offer to take that person in. The timing may be inconvenient. You may dislike or even distrust the person. It doesn't matter. This is a difficult land, in which travelers bear many hardships. If those who seek food, rest, and shelter are turned away, the prevailing customs among people will not work for anyone

To amplify this tradition, the Jewish scriptures tell four stories of people who open their doors to strangers and find themselves entertaining angels unawares. In the most memorable story, three men turn up at the doorstep of Abraham and Sarah, who welcome them generously and without reservation. The strangers turn out to be messengers from God, who have come to tell the couple that Sarah, long unable to conceive, will now have a child. We never know whether the person on our doorstep will bring us new birth or new trouble. The storyteller thinks it's worth taking a chance.

This is a pretty radical concept for our world. When the doorbell rings, we frequently check a window first to determine how much of the door we should open or if we should open it at all. "Caller ID" helps us decide whether to pick up the phone. Our personal privacy, along with concern for our safety, is the overriding principle that determines who gets into our home. We extend hospitality to our friends without risk, but guard ourselves against unexpected intrusions—thereby excluding those who might bring unexpected blessings.

This passage goes further and asks us to entertain, even welcome, a world that must have seemed as alien then as it does now. It asks that we remember prisoners not just dutifully or even thoughtfully but as though we were "in prison with them." We are to remember those undergoing torture as if we were being tortured ourselves, bearing their pain. We are to give up our craving for wealth and be content with what we have. Could the passage have located three more sensitive subjects than torture, voluntary poverty, and welcoming prisoners? We are to be open enough to receive much of the pain and joy of the world without being protected by society's traditional safeguards—wealth, ignorance, locked doors.

This seems like a risky plan, but the alternative is leading a lesser life, a life guarded by everything that can protect, isolate, and smother. It is to live so carefully screened and protected that we never encounter angels in disguise or anyone else who isn't safe. And so we spend our time lamenting that God, good fortune, or life's many good gifts have not gotten past the barricades we have so carefully built around us.

Faith Without Works Is Dead

What good is it, my brothers and sisters, if you say you have faith but do not have works? Can faith save you? If a brother or sister is naked and lacks daily food, and one of you says to them, "Go in peace; keep warm and eat your fill," and yet you do not supply their bodily needs, what is the good of that? So faith by itself, if it has no works, is dead.

But someone will say, "You have faith and I have works." Show me your faith apart from your works, and I by my works will show you my faith. You believe that God is one; you do well. Even the demons believe—and shudder. Do you want to be shown . . . that faith apart from works is barren?

JAMES 2:14–20

It can be hard, if not impossible, to know when we are doing the right thing, when our lives are headed in the right direction. We worry constantly about our performance, and we too often wonder how we rate compared to others. How do we reassure ourselves? Nothing works entirely, but in Western culture there are two traditional pathways by which people come to believe they are doing the right thing.

Some say that if your faith in God is true and unwavering, God will respond by bringing blessings into your life, and your passage through the pearly gates will be assured. Therefore, do not worry about accomplishments; simply believe without ceasing, and God will be content.

Others, like the author of this passage, believe the only true test of your faith and loyalty is your accomplishments in fulfilling God's will for humankind. Faith by itself is laudable, but if it accomplishes nothing on earth, it is also meaningless. A faith that does not feed the hungry or clothe the naked is false and self-serving. It does not build churches and synagogues or contribute to peace on earth. We need to witness and work for what we believe.

However, there comes a point when enough work is enough, and that's why the issues of faith and works are linked in this passage. Our need for accomplishment is so great that we never quite know when to stop working. We drive ourselves mercilessly, completing one project after another, advancing one small step at a time as if the goal of our lives is to get straight "As" in everything.

Jesus certainly never believed that we should spend our lives piling up earthly credits. He taught quite otherwise. But he would also have agreed that love of God without regard to God's particular concern for suffering humanity would be a limp faith, yielding little satisfaction or happiness. And he would have told us that when we finally believe God's goodness is real, we will be more willing to serve others out of our own generosity of spirit and can be more giving to ourselves. Our inability to be generous is at the heart of what troubles modern men and women. In our times it has never really been a question of living only by faith or only by works. The question is when we will develop enough faith in God, life, and ourselves to know when to stop working.

The Parable of the Laborers
in the Vineyard

For the kingdom of heaven is like a landowner who
went out early in the morning to hire laborers for his
vineyard. After agreeing with the laborers for the usual
daily wage, he sent them into his vineyard. When he
went out about nine o'clock, he saw others standing
idle in the marketplace; and he said to them, "You
also go into the vineyard, and I will pay you whatever is right." So they went. When he went out again
about noon and about three o'clock, he did the same.
And about five o'clock he went out and found others
standing around; and he said to them, "Why are you
standing here idle all day?" They said to him, "Because
no one has hired us." He said to them, "You also go
into the vineyard." When evening came, the owner of
the vineyard said to his manager, "Call the laborers and
give them their pay, beginning with the last and then
going to the first." When those hired about five o'clock

came, each of them received the usual daily wage. Now when the first came, they thought they would receive more; but each of them also received the usual daily wage. And when they received it, they grumbled against the landowner, saying, "These last worked only one hour, and you have made them equal to us who have borne the burden of the day and the scorching heat." But he replied to one of them, "Friend, I am doing you no wrong; did you not agree with me for the usual daily wage? Take what belongs to you and go; I choose to give to this last the same as I give to you. Am I not allowed to do what I choose with what belongs to me? Or are you envious because I am generous?" So the last will be first, and the first will be last.

MATTHEW 20:1–16

How would you feel if you had been working in the broiling sun for twelve hours, and at the end of that time the man who hired you paid you the wage he had promised, but then he also paid the same amount to workers who had waltzed in an hour ago and hadn't even worked up a sweat? You would say, "That's unfair," as did the workers in this parable that Jesus tells. The ideal of fairness is something that unites all of us: saints and sinners. Even thieves, I suppose, look for fairness in the distribution of their ill-gotten loot.

Fairness is one of the first things we learned when we were growing up. It was the reason given why we could or could not have something we wanted. It was also the principle by which we sometimes overcame our parent's objections. It was the way we learned that we have rights over which other children are not allowed to trespass and even some rights we could assert with teachers. Fairness became the rock-bottom principle of our lives. We believed in it more than we believed in anything else.

When I was a camp counselor one of the most trying tests of my skill came on the one night a week when the kitchen served pie. A large round apple or blueberry pie was delivered to the center of each table and the counselor was charged with dividing it up into ten equal pieces. Never has the counselor been the focus of such intense scrutiny not to mention instruction. You could tell when the pie had reached the table because every child was off his bench and leaning in one direction. All heads clustered in a circle around the pie. The counselor was tracing faint lines in the pie crust trying to convince his campers that all final decisions would be fair and equal. But of course without scientific instruments, that would have been impossible.

However, because of how we react in groups even when great efforts have been made to avoid unfairness, someone will perceive it anyway. One counselor finally got so annoyed with this wrangling over centimeters of pie that he took a fork and scrambled the pie into what looked like a blueberry stew. His point was: It's the same pie, only now you don't have to fight over it.

This parable turns our preoccupation with fairness around so that we look at it critically. We count on fairness, and we are sometimes quick to perceive unfairness, but this story implies that it's not about fairness; it's about generosity. Strangely enough, fairness and generosity can be at odds with each other. Fairness is often a game of inches that humans play, but the parable may suggest that it is not God's game. It is not God's concern. In the kingdom of which Matthew is speaking (and it's not clear whether that kingdom is in heaven or on earth), everyone will be loved and given to equally and generously, because that is what God chooses to do. Fairness will not be an issue.

What if we go at the story from the point of view of the vineyard owner? If he pays everyone the same wage regardless of how much work he gets from them, he won't stay in business very long. The analogy doesn't hold, however, and that may be the point. We are measuring the vineyard owner in human terms, and we measure God in the same way, with our limitations and motivations. God is infinitely more giving than we are.

The Parable of the Sower of Seeds

When a great crowd gathered and people from town after town came to him, he said in a parable: "A sower went out to sow his seed; and as he sowed, some fell on the path and was trampled on, and the birds of the air ate it up. Some fell on the rock; and as it grew up, it withered for lack of moisture. Some fell among thorns, and the thorns grew with it and choked it. Some fell into good soil, and when it grew, it produced a hundredfold." As he said this, he called out, "Let anyone with ears to hear listen!"

LUKE 8:4-8

Imagine you are having a conversation with four friends, and you tell them something that is really important to you. What you have to say speaks to the heart of who you are and what you believe.

The first friend takes issue with what you are saying before you express even half of it. The last thing you expected was a debate, but he seems intent on shattering your thought upon the grounds of logical or empirical analysis. The second friend doesn't really hear you at all, doesn't understand where you are going with the thought because he isn't really listening. It is as if your seeds are falling on rock and rolling right off. The third friend does understand some of what you are saying but relates it so much to her own particular obsessions that she distorts your thought into her own. In the end, this topic is so important to you that it gets caught up in thorns and cannot be freed.

The fourth friend listens very carefully and asks some questions to make sure she understands what you mean. She then repeats back what she thinks she has learned from you. Finally, after pausing to reflect, she responds in a way that makes you feel truly heard. Her response may not be complete agreement, but she makes it clear that something genuine and important to both of you has passed between you.

It would probably be a mistake to characterize the first three listeners as insensitive people whom we would rather not have in our lives. At various times, we have had all three of them in our lives, for they are us. We, too, can spring into debate mode, all too quick to pound a friend's feelings into the ground. We can be magnificently deaf even to the people we love. We also can become so enthralled with our own issues that we hear everything as a reflection of our own issues rather than a word from someone else's heart.

The truth of our lives is that active listening may not be the mode we revert to most often when we are with other people. It takes an act of self consciousness and self discipline to be genuinely with someone else. In the parable, Jesus concludes, "Let anyone with ears to hear listen," but, of course, it is not a question of hearing alone. It is a question of being authentically present with minds, hearts, and feelings, and engaged in receiving another person. It's how we want to be. It is not always, maybe not even often, how we are. Perhaps the images of this parable will help us to act out of our best selves.

The Parable of the Good Samaritan

Just then a lawyer stood up to test Jesus. "Teacher," he said, "what must I do to inherit eternal life?" He said to him, "What is written in the law? What do you read there?" He answered, "You shall love the Lord your God with all your heart, and with all your soul, and with all your strength, and with all your mind; and your neighbor as yourself." And he said to him, "You have given the right answer; do this, and you will live."

But wanting to justify himself, he asked Jesus, "And who is my neighbor?" Jesus replied, "A man was going down from Jerusalem to Jericho, and fell into the hands of robbers, who stripped him, beat him, and went away, leaving him half dead. Now by chance a priest was going down that road; and when he saw him, he passed by on the other side. So likewise a Levite, when he came to the place and saw him, passed by on the other side. But a Samaritan while traveling came near him; and when he saw him, he was moved with pity. He went to him and bandaged his wounds, having poured oil and wine on them. Then he put him on his own animal, brought him to an inn, and took care of him. The next day he took out two denarii, gave them to the innkeeper, and said, Take care of him; and when I come back, I will repay you whatever more you spend. Which of these three, do you think, was a neighbor to the man who fell into the hands of the robbers?" He said, "The one who showed him mercy." Jesus said to him, "Go and do likewise."

LUKE 10:25–37

We can identify with this story. We can identify with the traveler who, lying beaten and naked by the side of the road, is as vulnerable as anyone could be. He cannot help himself, and if someone does not help him, he will die. He sees a priest, a religious man, coming down the road and his spirits soar. "Surely," thinks the traveler, "this man will take it as his religious duty to help me." But the priest walks by, pretending not to see him.

The next person down the road is a Levite. Once more the traveler's hopes are raised, because a Levite is a "better sort of person." But the Levite walks by as well. The traveler is pretty nearly desperate, thinking of death, when he sees another figure coming out of the haze. Again his hopes rise, but then he recognizes the person as a Samaritan. This is a group of people that Jews, like this traveler, have scorned. Surely this new stranger will not stop to help a Jew. Yet, amazingly, he does help. He tends to the man's wounds, places the traveler on his own animal, and takes him to an innkeeper. He then promises to pay the innkeeper the full cost of caring for the traveler when he returns.

The Samaritan's next actions are worth noting or they wouldn't have been mentioned in the story. He does not stop to be thanked or congratulated or to explain his actions. He doesn't wait to find out how much the bill might be. Whatever it is, he will pay it. The Samaritan is not as impressed with his own goodness as we have been. He acted out of compassion because it seemed the right thing to do. After rendering aid and probably saving the traveler's life, he moved on with his own business.

Like most parables, this story is freighted with meanings. One of these may be that persons holding religious and cultural offices (the priest and Levite) do not in every instance act with compassion. Probably no one does in every instance. We can't tell how much someone will act as a neighbor based on their rank. Nor can we assume that all Samaritans are inherently generous. They're probably no more or less generous than any other people. Everyone is a potential "Samaritan." Everyone, regardless of rank, role, or outward prestige, is a potential neighbor. We need to look at one another with that kind of hope and expectation and try to fulfill it in ourselves.

It is also helpful to look at the situation from the viewpoint of the priest or Levite. The original hearers of this story would have known that the priest and the Levite had religious reasons for not stopping to touch what they might have thought to be a dead body. We have all been in this story more than once. We have passed by people who were in distress. We did it because we thought they didn't deserve help, they were faking their distress. We decided we couldn't have helped them much anyway or we were in too much of a hurry or preoccupation with our own issues. We make these decisions almost daily and without much thought. Some have coined the term *compassion fatigue* to describe the point at which many of us turn a deaf ear to the pleas of beaten travelers.

In its very basic form, this story reminds us that we have been in the roles of the priest, the Levite, and the beaten traveler, and some of us have been in the role of the Samaritan. What is it that brings the Samaritan forth in us? As is true with many of Jesus' parables, we must find that answer in our own hearts.

The Parable of the Man Who Threw a Banquet

Then Jesus said to him, "Someone gave a great dinner and invited many. At the time for the dinner he sent his slave to say to those who had been invited, 'Come; for everything is ready now.' But they all alike began to make excuses. The first said to him, 'I have bought a piece of land, and I must go out and see it; please accept my regrets.' Another said, 'I have bought five yoke of oxen, and I am going to try them out; please accept my regrets.' Another said 'I have just been married, and therefore I cannot come.' So the slave returned and reported this to his master. Then the owner of the house became angry and said to his slave, 'Go out at once into the streets and lanes of the town and bring in the poor, the crippled, the blind, and the lame.' And the slave said, 'Sir, what you have ordered has been done, and there is still room.' Then the master said to the slave, 'Go out into the roads and lanes, and compel people to come in, so that my house may be filled.'"

LUKE 14:16–23

Imagine that you gave a lavish dinner party and no one came. It could happen. Most people worry that it will happen. When you give a dinner or host any event, you put yourself "out there." You run the risk of not getting the guests you hoped for or getting the wrong mix for conversation. The meal could turn out poorly or the chemistry between guests might not be right. In our world—and in the world of the gospels—the simple, wonderful act of offering hospitality can cause anxiety and embarrassment.

The man in this parable risked a great deal, for he proposed to give a large dinner and he "invited many." As was the custom, when the time for the meal came around, he sent forth his slave a second time to tell his guests the meal was ready. Suddenly he began to hear what sounded like thin excuses for begging off the invitation. One man had to go out and look at land he just bought. (It couldn't wait?) Another had to try out a pair of oxen he just bought. (They couldn't wait? The oxen had another appointment?) And the third man might have mentioned before that he was about to get married.

This party is now about to be a social disaster. One by one, the rich man's guests offered transparent reasons for not accepting his hospitality. If we were in the rich man's shoes, we might have gone to the "B" guest list and hoped to fill the party that way. Perhaps we would cancel the party, and then rent a movie, or go out for Chinese, hoping that word of our embarrassment would not travel too far and wide.

Instead, this man would not allow himself to be embarrassed, shamed, or humiliated by the actions of other people. He sends his servant out to invite the poor, the crippled, the blind, and the lame. "Bring them all in," he seems to say, "for they will surely enjoy this feast that has been prepared." He wants to have a party. He wants to share his blessings. He wants to know that others appreciate his hospitality, and by God, that's what he's going to do—social stigma or humiliation be damned.

This is the story of a man who would not be daunted by social convention. He wanted to give a banquet. He wanted to share his wealth with others. If the "nice" people could not be bothered to attend, the man was more than happy to share his wealth with everyone. The story reminds us that generosity is a trait that is wonderful, transforming, and all too rare. As we receive daily evidence of God's blessings upon everyone, our lives are strengthened and our days lightened.

The Parable of the Prodigal Son

Then Jesus said, "There was a man who had two sons. The younger of them said to his father, 'Father, give me the share of the property that will belong to me.' So he divided his property between them. A few days later the younger son gathered all he had and traveled to a distant country, and there he squandered his property in dissolute living. When he had spent everything, a severe famine took place throughout that country, and he began to be in need. So he went and hired himself out to one of the citizens of that country, who sent him to his fields to feed the pigs. He would gladly have filled himself with the pods that the pigs were eating; and no one gave him anything. But when he came to himself he said, 'How many of my father's hired hands have bread enough and to spare, but here I am dying of hunger! I will get up and go to my father, and I will say to him, "Father, I have sinned against heaven and before you; I am no longer worthy to be called your son; treat me like one of your hired hands.'" So he set off and went to his father. But while he was still far off, his father saw him and was filled with compassion; he ran and put his arms around him and kissed him. Then the son said to him, 'Father, I have sinned against heaven and before you; I am no longer worthy to be called your son.' But the father said to his slaves, 'Quickly, bring out a robe—the best one—and put it on him; put a ring on his finger and sandals on his feet. And get the fatted calf and kill it, and let us eat and celebrate; for this son of mine was dead and is alive again; he was lost and is found!' And they began to celebrate.

"Now his elder son was in the field; and when he came and approached the house, he heard music and dancing. He called one of the slaves and asked what was going on. He replied 'Your brother has come, and your father has killed the fatted calf, because he has got him back safe and sound.' Then he became angry and refused to go in. His father came out and began to plead with him. But he answered his father, 'Listen! For all these years I have been working like a slave for you, and I have never disobeyed your command; yet you have never given me even a young goat so that I might celebrate with my friends. But when this son of yours comes back, who has devoured your property with prostitutes, you killed the fatted calf for him!' Then the father said to him, 'Son you are always with me, and all that is mine is yours. But we had to celebrate and rejoice, because this brother of yours was dead and has come to life; he was lost and has been found.'"

LUKE 15:11–32

Coming to us from almost two thousand years ago, this story has something to hook nearly everyone.

The elder son speaks for many when he says, in effect, "Father are you out of your mind!? I have been by your side through thick and thin for these many years, and I've never complained or asked for as much as a sliver of your money. Did I get even so much as a thanks or a small gift? No. Now my brother comes home, having disgraced himself and spent your money, but you kill the fatted calf and invite the neighbors in for a feast. What kind of gratitude is that!?"

The story also brings home many parental moments. Returning home on a night of bad weather, your child is late by an hour or more. You want to kill him. When he finally comes through the door safely, you want to hug him, but instead you merely ground him for a week. It also brings home all our sibling moments. Your brother is getting away with something you are sure you would never have been allowed to do—not that you would have done it yourself, of course—and you think justice should be served.

The story contradicts all of our normal reactions and suggests that neither punishment nor shaming is the real issue. This is not a justice issue either. What is most important is that the bonds of family and of community, which had been broken, can now be restored. Considering the "family feuds" that go on in many homes, this is a radically different priority, and it speaks of a radical notion of God. A traditional understanding of God is that of a judge who separates the good from the bad, the faithful from the unfaithful. This notion is reflected in some Jewish and Christian scriptures, but the much stronger Biblical witness is that God seeks connection and reconciliation and can more likely be experienced when we have made peace with one another.

The Parable of the Pharisee
and the Tax Collector

He also told this parable to some who trusted in themselves that they were righteous and regarded others with contempt: "Two men went up to the temple to pray, one a Pharisee and the other a tax collector. The Pharisee, standing by himself, was praying thus, 'God, I thank you that I am not like other people: thieves, rogues, adulterers, or even like this tax collector. I fast twice a week; I give a tenth of all my income.' But the tax collector, standing far off, would not even look up to heaven, but was beating his breast and saying, 'God, be merciful to me, a sinner!' I tell you, this man went down to his home justified rather than the other; for all who exalt themselves will be humbled, but all who humble themselves will be exalted."

LUKE 18:9–14

The key to this parable is understanding that a Pharisee was a person of power and influence in Jesus' time and the tax collector was a toady of the hated Roman occupiers. It would be too easy for us to hear this parable and think like the Pharisee. We have said of someone else, "I can't stand it that she is so judgmental of other people. Who does she think she is always finding fault, always comparing the success of others to her own?" Or we've thought that someone is a "stuffed shirt, so pretentious, so stuck on himself." Thinking these things, we thank God that we are not as other people are.

It is more honest to recognize that most of us are "as other people are." Sometimes we are even as the people we consider too judgmental. We begin to compare ourselves to others early in our lives: what they have learned, what they have achieved, what they own, how they look. We compare not only to assure ourselves we are "on track" but to find those who are less gifted in some areas and then feel good about our advantages over them. These kinds of comparisons become especially deadly if they begin to drive our lives as they do for many adults.

The tax collector side of us grows with maturity. We slowly realize that despite all the admirable qualities we have developed, we have a core anxiety about our worthiness as people. We are anxious to have a place in the world that is better than others have. Sometimes we act out of that anxiety more than anything else. We have a terrible need to be first. Often, we trip over this anxiety after we've acted impulsively, which we then regret for it has not shown us off well. We did not see our self-absorption until it poisoned a relationship we might have enjoyed.

In other words, we sin as well as succeed. This does not mean we abandon our self esteem. It means that we balance our self esteem by not taking ourselves too seriously. We recognize our potential to harm and try to keep it under firm control. We know how easily it can dominate our lives and other lives. If we recognize how often we cross the line between our best judgment and our worst instincts, we may do so less frequently. Knowing how easy it is to slip up and hurt someone is what it means to know that you are a sinner. We become better people for that knowledge.

Afterword

The Bible is an inspired work, but not because it is the literal word of God. It is the words of people who have reflected over the centuries on the journeys of life. The words have emerged after their writers walked paths of self discovery and committed to responsibilities far beyond their own private lives. These writings have filtered through the thoughts of thousands of teachers and editors, so that what remains reflects much of the inspiration of Western civilization. Whether this amounts to encountering the spirit of God is something for each reader to decide. Regardless of our beliefs, it is an encounter with writers who reflected on God.

We can look at the sixty passages cited here as a potential mirror of our own thoughts and feelings. They reflect what has been joyful or painful or meaningful to us. We can also use them as a window to experience the world as others do. Through them we can understand the suffering that lingers in every community; recognize our evasions and hypocrisies, perhaps for the first time; and challenge ourselves on the seriousness of our commitments.

Like Cain, we have sometimes felt unappreciated and abused.

Like Jacob, we have wrestled with our angels. Like the psalmist, we have been caught in a net of conflicting commitments that we ourselves created. Like the religious leaders on the road to Jerusalem, we have passed by on the other side, refusing to help the stricken traveler. Like the elder son in Jesus' parable, we have resented what felt like the undeserved good fortune of others. These passages link us with a world of fellow pilgrims as well as spiritual advisers who are, like it or not, part of our religious family.

Readers who have enjoyed this book might want to take a further step. Give careful thought to the passages that you most liked—whether because of or in spite of my reflections. What appealed to you about these passages? This is where the Bible becomes a mirror, reflecting the nature of our personal religious faith, however inarticulate it may still be for us.

Next, give careful thought to the passages you found most troubling. What are you reacting to? What troubles, saddens, or angers you? Make a list as well of those passages you found most difficult to understand. Try to become aware of where you are getting caught and why. Often, what troubles us most points us toward the path we eventually need to follow.

To continue the work of this book you may wish to join a Bible discussion group—one that assumes there are no right answers and has as its goal the growth of each participant, rather than the molding of each to one point of view. You may want to enter into the ongoing conversation by reading commentary and reflections about these passages. There are many resources out there, of course, and you will have to find the writers or preachers that most speak to you.

Finally, the longer you reflect on the scriptures the more likely it is that the ways in which you hear some of the passages will change. Some things will stand out that you never noticed earlier. Some passages that trouble you will become clearer, and some passages that seemed perfectly clear can become more complex.

This struggle to understand ourselves and others through the scriptures will not let us go. But if we wrestle with them long enough, they will become a blessing.